Eight Acres and a Cow

EIGHT ACRES AND A COW

CAROL RICHARDSON

proving
press

Book Design & Production
Columbus Publishing Lab
www.ColumbusPublishingLab.com

Paperback ISBN: 978-1-63337-268-9
E-book ISBN: 978-1-63337-269-6

Printed in the United States of America
1 3 5 7 9 10 8 6 4 2

Eight Acres and a Cow is dedicated to my four grandchildren, Jonah, Raul, Caroline and Ellie, and to my parents, Roscoe Edwin Richardson and Eva Pearl Johnson Richardson.

Prologue

I didn't want to move to Ohio—it was flat, it was ugly, and it didn't have crawdads in the creeks. Or that's what I had decided. The North Carolina mountains were home, and that's where I wanted to stay. But we Richardsons had to pack up our boxy old car and drive two days so Daddy could find work. That's where this grandma tale begins. The story happened about seventy years ago when I was a kid, when growing up was very different from now. As best I can remember it, I will tell you what it was like. Here we go . . .

Leap but No Frogs

We sat in the car, staring out the window at a shabby little house hidden back in the trees. It looked even worse than I had feared. The "new place," as Mom called it, was a dirty red brick—an Ohio house—a no-front-porch house. At the farm in North Carolina we'd had a spot for neighbors to come sit and visit. In no-porch Ohio we had nowhere to swing, nowhere to watch lightning bugs, nowhere to rock and snap beans and talk softly into the night. It was a bad start.

But big brother Jerry already had ideas about Ohio fun even without a front porch. As soon as the car came to a stop, he sprang open the door and bolted like a rabbit from a cage. No one was surprised. Jerry often launched himself without warning. It was his way, like firecrackers were exploding inside him. I preferred to give my eyes and ears a chance to work before I started my legs.

I took in the long front yard of the Ohio house. It stretched, dry and dreary, from the not-a-real-porch front stoop to the gravel road. At the end of the cinder drive, a mailbox perched like a vulture on a splintery post, its gloomy metal head thrust out hungrily and vigilantly over the road. Leap Road it was called, and when I'd first heard the name back in North Carolina, I had pictured frogs. *If Ohio has frogs*, I had thought, *maybe it won't be so bad*. But with the reality in front of me, I quickly determined that Leap Road had no porch, no creek, and no frogs.

"Those trees will make good shade, Eva." Daddy peered out the window. Giant elm trees stood leafy guard over the house, and two sparkling boulders rolled up tight against their base. Mom nodded approval. "And that looks like rich dirt for a garden." Daddy pointed to a big open space that ran along the side of the house. He was trying hard to make the bad into good.

Daddy never said it, but I knew he didn't want to leave North Carolina either. He had grown up on a farm there. He was at home in the mountains—Mom too, but in the West Virginia mountains that had black coal for bones, miners who dug it, and long, slow trains that hauled it away.

But there were no jobs in West Virginia or North Carolina, and, "You got to go where the work is," Daddy had said. Of course, Mom had agreed, so here we were, transplanted to Ohio and aching for our mountain home.

A wire fence marked the property line by the drive. Both the fence and the drive curled around the garage to the back. Jerry reappeared from that direction, his firecrackers still bursting like the Fourth of July.

"Well, Eva, we better get inside before Jerry fires off again," Daddy chuckled. "You ready to see our new house, Sweet Potato?" Daddy turned his brave smile on me and pushed open the heavy car door.

I saw how tired he was and how ready he was to be done with the trip. We all were. We had traveled nearly two days up, down, and around on the twisty mountain roads through North Carolina, Virginia, and West Virginia. We had forded creeks and streams on narrow, one-car-at-a-time bridges. We had camped overnight by the side of the road and peed in the woods in every state we crossed. When we got to Wheeling in West Virginia, an iron bridge curved from bank to bank over the Ohio River into our new home state. Columbus was straight west from Wheeling with no mountains in between, but it still took forever to finish the trip. We had sputtered along in our old gray Dodge for more than 500 miles. We had come from a hill-and-valley farm in western North Carolina to a little brick house in the flat middle of Ohio, and we were worn down to the nub.

The Cut

Daddy had wanted to travel on the weekend. "Less traffic," he reasoned. "And I have to start the new job on Monday." So early Saturday morning we gathered last hugs from Grandma and Grandpa and waved final goodbyes. Daddy pressed the starter of the cranky old Dodge, then eased its gray hulk down the dirt path away from the farmhouse. At the bottom of the hill, we rumbled over the boards laid across Crawdad Creek and strained up the final stretch of gravelly hill. Daddy stopped at the top to shift gears. We pulled onto the main road, and as we made the turn, I caught a glimpse of the trailer that bumped along behind. The headboard from my bed banged against the low, open sides, and an oilcloth table covering flapped in the wind.

The Dodge turned west toward Nigger Mountain, which was still part of Richardson land. Grandpa always said

11

runaway slaves used to hide up on that mountain until they could slip away in the night and head north and get free. When the white folks found out, Grandpa said, they'd set the coon dogs loose on the mountain to hunt them down. "Them hounds would go all night, an' ya knowed when they caught one of them nigger runaways, 'cause the dogs'd go crazy barkin.'"

That was the Nigger Mountain story, and I guess it was true because Great Grandpa owned the land the mountain was on, and maybe he set his coon dogs loose. Grandpa never said, but I suspected it was so.

I liked North Carolina stories, but never that one. The whole thing was bad from beginning to end. For starters, people can't own another person like they're an animal or something. It's just flat-out wrong. Any person with an ounce of sense knows that. And coon hounds? Well, they're good-size dogs, and they could grab hold and tear a person up pretty bad. So that part was just plain mean. The wicked slave owning and the hateful dog thing were cruel enough, but the mountain's name was ugly too. And worse, when people told the story, they used that hateful name for the people who ran away. Mom said "nigger" was not a word she wanted coming out of her children's mouths even if it did come out of their grandpa's. Mom was strong on the subject.

The mountain loomed over us as the car covered the five miles into town and slowly ground its way onto West

Jefferson's main street. There wasn't much to the town, really, just a line of stores and a few houses backed up to the
hillside. We passed the grocery and dry goods stores and the
Asheland Bank, where Daddy would go to pay on the loan at
the end of every month. We crept by the hardware and feed
stores, not yet open for the day.

The town also had a jailhouse. It was in the same building as the post office, where the townspeople went most days
to check for mail. Folks dropped letters through the slot,
bought a penny stamp or postcard when they needed one,
and traded gossip with Edna, perched on her stool behind
the window. Edna knew pretty much everything that went
on in town, and you could count on her to tell it, plus other
stuff she didn't know anything about and wasn't any of her
business. Or that's what Mom always said.

"Keep your eyes peeled," Daddy said. "We got to pick
up The Cut on the other side of town." The Cut was an oiled
gravel road that cut up and over the mountain range. It was
the shortest route to the other side where we would take the
state road north.

The entrance to The Cut was unmarked and veered
sharply up the mountain. Logging trucks used it to haul new
cut timber down to the main road. Taking the shortcut over
the mountain was tricky and required good timing because
the narrow road was barely wide enough for two cars to
pass, let alone a car and a truck loaded with thirty-foot logs

chained to its bed. A car going up did not want to meet a logging truck coming down.

Mom didn't like The Cut. "Too dangerous," she said. "You never know when the logging trucks are coming." Daddy agreed, but the timber foreman had assured him that they wouldn't be running any loads down on Saturday.

"Besides," Daddy pointed out, "taking the shortcut over the mountains will save us hours on the road." Mom didn't argue with that.

Jerry spotted The Cut entrance ahead, and Daddy geared into second. The Dodge needed the extra power for the sharp rise up from the main road. Immediately, shadowy branches swallowed us, and we entered the mountain solitude. The gravel route rose before us and curled like an oily rope, pulling us through the trees.

The gray Dodge bumped steadily along for a half hour or more, leaving behind a thin trail of dust puffs. Mom and Daddy rode in tense silence, and I hardy moved in the back seat. Even Jerry's firecrackers were quiet. Despite the assurance of the timber foreman, no one could relax. All our eyes strained forward up the mountainside, and we scanned the road ahead for any sign of dirt clouds kicked up by a logging truck coming down.

"How much farther, Ross?" Mom's question jerked us from our concentration.

"We're almost to the ridge where they've been cutting,"

Daddy said. "We should be clear after that. No trucks go down on the other side, and no dust clouds ahead on this side." His voice was filled with relief.

But then a Monster sprang from nowhere. It roared over the hill and charged down upon us. Skinned logs shifted perilously on its back, and great clods of oiled gravel spewed from its tires. The terrible beast filled the road ahead. There was no escape.

I stopped breathing. Jerry braced his arms against the front seat in terror. Mom's hand held a scream in her mouth. The Monster's driver laid on the horn to sound a desperate warning, but he could not brake. It was too dangerous. His rig would fishtail and unleash his load of logs down the mountainside. The Dodge and the log truck would surely be swept over, along with everyone inside.

Only Daddy could save us, and I knew he would if he could. He yanked the Dodge sharply right, and the old car teetered on the knife edge of road and cliff. The Dodge shuddered. The trailer skittered. It wobbled dangerously and threatened to pull our car sideways over the sheer cliff to the valley below.

But both car and trailer held the gravel footing. Only the oilcloth table covering was lost as it tore loose from the mattress and sailed over the cliff as the truck careened by.

The Monster shrieked down the road and into the overhanging trees. It disappeared as mysteriously as it had appeared, and quiet surrounded us again as if it had never left. Daddy eased the car and trailer back onto the gravel and started the final climb up to the safety of the ridge. No one dared talk until we reached the top, but thankfully no more Monsters appeared.

The Picture Box

The Dodge bumped up one mountain and down another. I got tired of tedious stay-in-the-lines coloring, so I tried comic books but had already read them. It was way too early to eat, and Mom warned me not to drink too much or I wouldn't hold my pee. So I pulled out the road map and spread it across my lap to find the spot where we were and trace our trip.

The map opened and closed like a paper accordion, but very soon I got it crinkled and folded in all the wrong places. The state lines didn't connect anymore and steered off course in the paper crumples. In a matter of minutes, I transformed the neat rectangle of a map into another Monster that swallowed up the tiny words and sent the wiry road lines careening out of control.

"Want some help?" Jerry offered. He quickly refolded the map into a manageable square that showed a section of western North Carolina and some of Virginia. He pointed out West Jefferson, where the farm was, the stretch of mountains we had cut over, and the thin red line we were driving on. For once it was nice to have an older brother.

I gratefully reclaimed the map and traced my finger along the wavy string that was our route. Mom told me that Virginia was the next state. I wanted to know when we left North Carolina, so I watched for clues out the window, but trees and more trees rose up in the front windshield and fell behind in the rear. It all looked the same, and I figured I'd leave North Carolina and not even know it.

"The state line's right up ahead," Daddy announced. His voice jolted me from my disappointment. I leaned toward the window to get my last glimpse of my home state, but I still couldn't tell where it ended and Virginia began. The mountains ahead looked just like the mountains behind.

"Look there!" Mom pointed to a grand *Welcome to Virginia!* sign planted among the maples. Daddy pulled over into a cleared parking area just past the welcome sign. Three other cars were already there. Their people had climbed out and were standing in the open to stretch and twist the car kinks away. Some wandered to the fenced edge of the overlook to peer out at the tops of Virginia trees and at the fog that hovered over a tiny town below in the valley. Daddy headed to the outhouse over the hill, and Mom stood with Jerry and me to take in the view.

"Okay, line up over there under the welcome sign," Mom directed after everyone had taken an over-the-hill turn. She had the Kodak box camera hanging around her neck, ready to shoot the first stop on the way to our new Ohio home.

"Hold still, Jerry." Daddy laid a calming hand on Jerry's shoulder.

"Okay, get ready." Mom lifted the Kodak's cover flap. She studied the image in the preview window and then stepped forward to fill the screen. "Still not right." She shifted left. "I can't get you all in." She held the camera steady in both hands at her waist. "Hold it," she pleaded. Jerry twitched, I froze, and Daddy did his best to keep smiling. Mom bowed her head to study the image one last time; then she pushed the shutter lever with her thumb. The Kodak made a double click as the lens opened and closed like a one-eyed frog.

"Come on, Eva. We gotta get you in the picture too." Daddy stepped out of line. Jerry's firecrackers resisted the ordeal of standing still again, and he groaned in protest as Daddy changed places with Mom.

"Hope these turn out," Mom said as she reclaimed the camera. She folded down the Kodak lid to protect the glass. Mom's photography was a family joke. Sometimes she aimed too low and cut off all our heads, or aimed too high and got nothing but heads. She'd chop bodies in half or shoot a dangling arm without a body. Our Picture Box was full of disembodied limbs and headless people, but we never thought to throw them away.

Mom's taking pictures got me thinking, and before we got back on the road, I begged Daddy to pull the Picture Box out of the trunk. At first he resisted. "Nah, Sweet Potato. It's packed in there real tight."

But in the end my argument won out. "Please, please, Daddy, I'm just so tired of riding and I need something to do." With a bit of rearranging in the trunk, out came the big shoe box that held years of family photos. As the old Dodge lumbered back onto the Virginia road, I opened up the treasure trove. Right on top was a dog-eared black and white of Daddy and Mom on their honeymoon at Blowing Rock in North Carolina. They looked really young standing together beside an old funny-looking car.

"That's what cars looked like back in the 1920s," Mom remembered. "It ran good, but the seats were hard." In the picture, Mom leaned against the car's back fender, and Daddy had his foot hoisted onto the running board. Mom wore a stylish hat that sat cockeyed on her head and a skinny skirt that dropped below her knees. Her long-sleeve jacket had a wide collar that opened in a V at the throat and cinched tight at the waist to flare over her hips. I looked at the photo a long time. The Mom I knew always wore cotton-print housedresses and an apron. What had happened to the jaunty hat and slinky suit?

The next picture in the stack was even older. It was a shot of Daddy as a kid. Four shirtless boys sat sheepishly on a bedraggled goat. The boys' bare feet dragged on the dusty ground. I flipped the picture over and saw "Ross, Kemp, Tam, Fred—1913" penciled on the back.

"Ross is Daddy, of course." Mom answered my question. "And Kemp and Tam are his brothers—your uncles—and Fred is cousin Fred Roberts, Grandma's brother's boy." I knew them as big, burly men—all except Tam. He had been killed in a car accident. "Drunk," Mom once told me. "What a waste," she added. In the picture they were still just boys having fun.

I dug around in the box for more Richardson family photos and found one of Grandma in the farm's backyard. "Look at this one!" I passed the picture to Jerry. Grandma stood triumphant beside the chopping stump. She had a short-handled axe in one hand and a headless rooster upside down by his legs in the other.

"Guess he crossed her," figured Jerry. Any rooster that spurred Grandma ended up as Sunday dinner. Roosters were fast, but Grandma was faster.

I pulled out a photo of a tall, lean Grandpa standing outside the jailhouse/post office in West Jefferson. He didn't wear a badge or anything to show he was a deputy sheriff, but I knew he had locked up folks sometimes. I searched and found a few other frayed pictures of Grandma and Grandpa. They never smiled into the camera.

Mom's relatives always smiled. The family was big—ten girls and three boys—so the Picture Box was full of the "Johnson Clan," as Mom called them. Uncle Walter wore an army uniform in a shot taken when he was fighting in WWII. Mom's "Poppy" leaned on a shovel in front of a steam engine. Mom always bragged that he had been a railroader and an important man in Crumpler, West Virginia.

"He had that Johnson Eye," Mom laughed. "If he gave you 'the eye,' you knew you better quit what you were doing. But I was his favorite." Mom smiled over the front seat. "Everyone—even Mommy—said I could get whatever I wanted from him."

I pulled out another picture, and Mom began, "Now Mommy, she was big on church. Still is. When we were comin' up, seems like she was either gone off to a preachin' or layin' up in bed with another new baby. She expected us older ones to take care of the young ones. And that's what we did. End of story." Mom wasn't a big talker. Her mommy in the picture had hair parted in the middle and thick braids circling into a pile on her head. Her smile slid to the side where one corner lifted higher than the other. I put Mom's mommy back in the box.

I came to some newer photos done by real photographers. Mom said guys with cameras had gone door to door taking pictures for money. One shot was Jerry on a pony wearing his boots and a cowboy hat. Another showed me as a baby, sitting cross-legged on a bench. My curly blond hair fuzzed out around my face, and my crossed "lazy eye" showed up even then. I tucked that picture deep into the stack.

And there was a big photo of Norma. She was Daddy and Mom's other daughter. Norma had been beautiful—I could see it in the picture—and smart in school, Mom said. I knew Norma had gotten a brain tumor when she was ten, and it killed her. The doctors operated to take the tumor out, but Norma died anyway. Mom said that the cancer grew right back after the surgery, so there was no way to save her.

In the picture, Norma stood in a lacy striped dress with delicate lavender flowers, and she had a dainty silver ring on her little finger. I knew where the striped dress was, and the silver ring too. Both were in the cedar chest. The dress was carefully folded, and the ring was in a tiny gold jewelry box. Mom kept them there in the chest almost like Norma was coming back to wear them. Of course she wasn't, and wouldn't, and Mom knew that, but I guess she still wanted a miracle even if it couldn't be.

Daddy said Norma had been nine when the picture was taken. That was a year before she got sick. In the picture, Norma tipped her head sideways over her shoulder like she was walking away and looking back. Norma had died before Jerry or I was born, but whenever I came to her photographs in the Picture Box, I studied them. Why did little girls— beautiful, smart girls—get sick and die? And if a bad thing happened once in a family, could it happen again?

Hilliard

Mom worried about a breakdown, but Daddy said the car would make it to Ohio. We stopped two more times so everyone could stretch their legs, and Mom and I walked into the woods to squat in the grass and pee while Daddy and Jerry stood with their backs turned, facing a tree. We were all so tired of the car, but we climbed back in. There was nothing to do but to keep moving.

After we crossed into West Virginia, Daddy pulled over for the night. "This okay, Eva?" he asked as he steered the Dodge into a grassy turnout just off the road. Mom nodded.

By then we were ready to dig into the sausage biscuits and especially the sugar cookies Mom had packed. Right before we had left, she had sent me to fetch four fat ones out of the jar in Grandma's pantry and wrap them in a cloth so they wouldn't dry out. I tasted those cookies in my head for miles.

We piled out of the car, and Mom directed me to gather dry sticks for a fire. *Yes!* I thought. *Finally I can roam.* I took my time, selected carefully, and finally came back with an armload of twigs all different sizes. I knew to collect some thin-as-a-match sticks to lay down first, some finger-thick sticks, then two fingers, then three. Mom dragged over a few big branches to put on last. She laid out our fire on top of the ashes that other families had left before us.

"Get the water jug out of the back, Jerry," Mom directed. "Carol, you set out the cups." Daddy arranged two logs close to the fire and upended a big stump for our table. "The fire's for coffee after supper and to knock the chill off," Mom said. "We won't cook on the road." We settled on the log seats to unwrap the cold biscuits with salty sausage patties inside.

"Nothing better!" Daddy smacked. "Tastes like North Carolina."

"Tastes like home," I put in softly, but no one noticed.

After the quick supper, Mom sent Jerry and me off to the Dodge to stretch out as best we could for the night. Jerry got the front and I climbed in back. I guessed Daddy and Mom would get the grass by the fire.

We headed out again at sunup because Daddy was eager to get on the road. He wanted to make the Ohio River by mid-morning and cross over into Ohio from West Virginia. "We make Wheeling, and we're almost to Leap Road," he joked. I remembered about the frog possibility.

Wheeling came and went, and went, and went. We drove on for hours, it seemed, and the farther we got from North Carolina, the flatter it was. By the time we rolled near Columbus, the mountains were long gone and even the foothills had flattened into treeless fields.

"Columbus is Ohio's capital city." Mom broke the silence. "And it's where you were born—White Cross Hospital it was." She turned to me. "But we left when you were so little you don't remember it." Mom knew Columbus well. "There wasn't any work in West Virginia, so I left and came to Columbus when I was old enough to be on my own." I knew the story, but she wanted to fill the space, so she kept talking. "I lived with your aunt Annie over on Buttles Avenue. She was the first one of us Johnsons to come north for a job. I got work right away with the phone company—took the streetcar downtown every day and went to the picture show every night. If we could scrape together a nickel for the ticket, we'd go." She laughed. Those had been fun times for Mom. "Later I met your daddy at a big dance hall out east of Columbus someplace." Mom and Daddy twinkled at each other, and Daddy picked up the story.

"Yep, I had my eye on your mother right away. We danced our first dance in December and got married in March. That's the first time we lived in Ohio," Daddy finished. Times had been good in the beginning, but I knew the hard times came. Daddy and Mom often talked about living through the Depression in Columbus when Daddy had no job. "No one could find any work," Daddy said, "and we had a baby to feed." The baby was Norma, of course, and that turned into the hardest thing of all when she died. Ohio had both good memories and bad for Mom and Daddy. After Norma, they started their family over again. Jerry was born the year after Norma died, and I came three years later. But Daddy's work petered out about that time, Mom said, so they had to "pull up stakes" in Columbus and head south. They hadn't planned to ever come back, but the Richardson family was moving to Columbus again because that was where the jobs were.

I had never been to any big city that I could remember, let alone a capital city, but from a distance Columbus didn't look like much, just two or three buildings stuck up into the sky.

"Hilliard is just ten miles more." Daddy was trying for upbeat.

Now you'd think a town named Hilliard would have some hills. But you'd be wrong. The last miles to our new home lay before us as thin and flat as a skimpy pancake. "Where are the Guernseys?" I searched out loud for something familiar, like buttery brown North Carolina cows. Ohio cows were all black-and-white Holsteins, including the three that quietly watched as we made the turn onto Leap Road.

◆◆◆

I woke up on the floor—well, actually on a mattress that was on the floor. We had gotten into our new house too late to put up the beds, so Daddy and Jerry hauled in the mattresses and plopped them down. Mom and I then dug around for sheets and blankets. That was pretty much all we got done before it was too dark to work. And everyone was glad for an excuse to quit.

On that first morning, it seemed like the sun came up earlier in Hilliard than on Grandpa and Grandma's farm. Probably the sun rose at the same time, but the rays had a direct and easy path through the windows since there were no mountains to climb over first.

Daddy and Mom were up early because it was Monday and Daddy was starting his new job. The Columbus Auto Parts Company plant was a ten-mile drive away, and his shift began at seven. "Breakfast fixins are pretty thin, Ross." I heard Mom's voice from the kitchen. "But at least there's some fresh coffee and leftover biscuits from the trip." Daddy said something I couldn't hear—maybe he told Mom not to worry, he'd get some groceries on the way home, he needed a list, he couldn't find his lunch pail. I liked their morning talk.

I stayed under the blanket until I heard the Dodge crank grudgingly and roll Daddy out onto Leap Road toward his first workday in a long time. When I couldn't hear the engine anymore, I wandered into the kitchen. Mom was sipping coffee. Quiet. Like always. Thinking. "Sleep okay?" she asked when she noticed I was there.

She was worn out, I could see it. Not just from the trip, but from all that had come before. Daddy had not had steady work for a long time. We had gone to North Carolina after leaving Ohio the first time, when I was too little to remember. But when we got there, there were no jobs, Mom said, so we drove on to Maryland. We stayed with Irene and Uncle Vinson while Daddy looked for work there. They lived right on the Chesapeake Bay, where the jobs were catching crabs or taking people charter fishing. But Daddy had been raised on a farm and didn't know about water jobs. It was no use staying in Maryland. Uncle George said to come to Virginia. He had found out about an opening at a feed store in Roanoke, something a farm boy like Daddy knew about. We went, but someone else got the job first. So we left Virginia to head for North Carolina again. Grandpa had told Daddy about work there making furniture. He got that job and we settled back on the farm.

I loved it. I think Jerry did too, and Daddy, because he was home again. But Mom did not get along with Grandma. You could feel that a squabble was just a sharp glance away. Mom tried hard to keep the peace, and she did her share of the chores and then some. Every morning she got up long before anyone else to build the fire in the kitchen stove. It had to be roaring hot to fry the sausage patties, make the gravy, and bake the biscuits. Even Grandma said Mom made the best biscuits.

But that was about all Grandma approved of. Nothing else Mom did was ever good enough. Mom's dresses didn't suit. Her apron had a spot. She didn't hang clothes on the line like she should. But the biggest disapproval was the cigarettes. Mom smoked sometimes and Grandma judged it "a dirty habit for a woman," and worse, "a sin."

"Your mother takes snuff," Mom said to Daddy in her own defense. "I don't see the difference." I tried to stay on the good side of both women, but in this I agreed with Mom. I knew Grandma kept snuff in her apron pocket. Off and on throughout the day, she'd open the little tin and slip a pinch of the powdery tobacco into her cheek. She thought she was being sneaky, but anyone could see the ugly tobacco spit in the corner cracks of her mouth. And it turned her teeth brown and made her breath sour. This seemed way dirtier than Mom's cigarettes. But I didn't say so.

I don't know if it was a good or a bad thing that the furniture place laid Daddy off. Good, I guess, because the meanness between Mom and Grandma was hard on us all. "Two women in the same house will surely cause trouble," Daddy said. But the layoff meant Daddy was out of work again, and that was bad.

Daddy left us on the farm and drove to Ohio where he'd heard there was work. He came back with the news that he had landed a millwright job for himself at the Columbus Auto Parts, and had rented a house for us on eight acres in the country. That's a sort of long story of how we got to Hilliard and why Mom looked so tired.

◆◆◆

"Ready for some breakfast?" Mom's question brought me back into the kitchen on Leap Road. "Not much here, but we'll make do until your daddy can get to the store over in town." The town part of Hilliard was a couple of miles away. Walkable for sure, but not that day when there were so many other things that had to be done.

"I'm not too hungry," I lied. "Cold biscuits would be good, and water."

"We've got a little jam." Mom smiled. "Grandma tucked a jar in with the trip food. It's strawberry." She held out the pint jar of home-canned jam. The paraffin seal still covered the top. I remembered the very day we had put up the batch. Grandma and I went out early to pick the berries from the patch down over the hill behind the house. Strawberries grew best in that spot, Grandma said, because the sun hit it just right. The plants were loaded down with clusters of ripe red goodness, and we picked all morning till it got too hot. Then the real work began: we washed, hulled, cooked, sugared, and mashed, then finally added the crab apple pectin to make the jam thicken. Grandma did the cooking part. I

31

washed jars and put them in the pot to boil the last germ dead. Grandma said the jam would spoil if we didn't do that part extra good.

When the hot jam was ready and the jars had no germs, Grandma filled each one almost to the rim and laid down a layer of melted paraffin over the top to harden and seal the jar. I was proud when we lined up two dozen jars of finished jam on the table for everyone to see.

Mom held up the brilliant red North Carolina jam for my first breakfast in the dingy Ohio-house kitchen. "Strawberry jam!" I put on a smile for Mom. I wanted the jam, but I was sad for the strawberry memory on the farm. I suspected the Ohio sun didn't shine right for strawberries.

After breakfast, Mom put Jerry and me to work unpacking boxes. We hung up coats and jackets in the upstairs wardrobe because we wouldn't be needing them until the weather got cold, and we put Daddy's work shirts and Mom's housedresses in the wardrobe down in the front room off the kitchen. Mom said they'd probably make that into a bedroom. Mom wiped down all the shelves in the little kitchen and used baking soda water to deodorize the icebox. Daddy would get a big chunk of ice on his way home, Mom said, and then we could keep our milk there so it wouldn't spoil so quick.

We hadn't had an icebox on the farm, just a spring house off the kitchen. Cool water from underground trickled through a trough there, and we would set milk and such in the trough to stay chilled. I was still thinking about the icebox wonder, but Mom was already scrubbing the stove.

"Where do you put the wood?" I asked her, searching for the door to the firebox.

"This stove doesn't take wood," she said. "It burns propane. See those tanks out there?" She pointed to two tall metal cylinders up against the house, just outside the window. "That's where the gas comes from to light the burners. I just need to find the matches." She searched through a box of kitchen supplies. "Ah, here they are." Mom held up a big box of Diamond kitchen matches. I'd never seen anything like this Ohio stove. On the farm, Daddy and Grandpa chopped wood that Jerry and I fetched from the pile to keep the woodbox full. Mom and Grandma used the kindling from the box to build a fire in the kitchen stove. We could fry eggs, roast chicken, boil dumplings—whatever we wanted. It had worked fine, but I quickly realized that the propane stove would sure cut down on the chopping and hauling work.

We kept at it all morning, cleaning, unpacking, and finding places to put things. I uncovered my drawing paper and crayons and the lined yellow tablet where I wrote down words that came to me. Mom called it my diary, but I thought of it more like a story book. It was full of my writing about things that happened to me or stories I just make up. I put both the drawing paper and my tablet with the box of crayons on a bookshelf in the new front room and added some pencils I found rolling around in the bottom of the moving box. My black-and-white Panda and brown Teddy with a tail were in the next box, but there was no bed to put them on yet. The shelf with the tablets had to do.

I heard Jerry going in and out of the house, banging the screen door every time. Firecrackers. And then it was lunchtime. Not much to eat on the table, but enough to get by. Mom made three-decker peanut butter cracker sandwiches, and she found a jar of peaches that we could share.

"Go fill the water jug," Mom told Jerry, and it was then that I realized there was no water in the spigot at the kitchen sink. The faucet was there, but it was dry. Jerry headed through the back door to an outdoor pipe and sloshed back in with the jug full. The Ohio house had no inside water. We wouldn't have to haul wood, but we would have to haul in every drop of water we used—water to drink, water to cook with, water to wash dishes, buckets full of water for the wash tubs and buckets more to take a bath. "Wash your hands." Mom pointed to a bar of soap at the kitchen sink and carefully poured a little stream from the jug to wet our hands.

We had made good progress in the morning. Mom had the dishes stacked and ready in the glass front cabinet, and I arranged the knives, forks, and spoons in the drawer underneath. The iron skillet sat on the stove, and other pans and lids were stored inside the oven. Mom had pinto beans soaking to cook for supper, but there would be no salt pork until Daddy got home from the store. I hoped for corn bread too, but Mom said not to because she didn't have buttermilk or eggs. "Maybe I can make some on Tuesday." Mom was tired. Supper would be dreary, but I didn't complain. Mom was doing her best.

"We worked so hard this morning; we deserve a break." Mom surprised us as we cleared the cracker plates and water glasses off the table. "Just put them in the sink. We'll boil some dishwater later. Let's get out a little." So we set off. We had eight acres to explore.

The back door opened into a dirt-floor garage that smelled like wet dogs, so we stepped quickly to the fresh air outside. A wire fence stretched across from one side of the lot to the other and separated the patch of grass close to the house from the field beyond. Another giant elm tree, sister to the ones in the front, shaded the entire backyard and then some. A smaller fruit tree flung its low branches over the house side of the fence. Maybe it was a pear tree or a cherry, but for sure it was a good climbing tree. An old, rusty pump stood just outside the garage. Jerry gave it a try, working the handle up and down furiously for a minute or two, but no water spurted out. Mom said the well must be dry, which was too bad because a well close to the kitchen door would have eased the water-hauling problem.

We followed the cinder drive through the wire gate

into the field. "Got to order coal before winter," Mom said as we passed a pile of black slag left from last year's coal. "That house is going to be hard to heat with just two stoves." Both heating stoves were cold in summer, but one sat in the bedroom where Daddy and Mom would sleep and the other in the front room where the davenport would go.

Blue chicory flowers lined the drive, and the grass was up to my waist. "Your daddy says we need a cow." Mom didn't sound so sure. I pictured one of those black-and-white Ohio jobs grazing on our eight acres. We ambled past the burn barrel for trash, which was directly across from the outhouse—a bad reminder that we had no inside water. On the farm, we had a working spigot in the kitchen and an inside bathroom off the hall. But not in Ohio.

"I hate outhouses," I mumbled.

"What?" Mom had heard.

"I hate outhouses," I said in a normal voice. "They always have spiders."

"So?" Jerry taunted, being big brother.

"So, spiders are creepy and they're always lurking in their webs with their little beady eyes watching me when I pee and stuff."

"And who knows when they might jump?" Jerry teased.

Or crawl or dangle down on me from a web string, I finished in my head. Sigh. Eventually I'd have to face down the creepy eight-leggers or I'd explode, but not yet. *I could just pee behind the bush in the backyard*, I thought, which was clearly preferable. I made it my plan to avoid the outhouse as often as possible.

The cinder path ended at a shed. Only half of it still stood, and the other half was a pile of boards fallen in on themselves. I quickly saw fun and climbed on top of the perilous pile to teeter on the planks. "Snakes," Mom said when she saw the haphazard stack of boards, and I reluctantly hopped back onto the grass. I knew to stay away, at least while Mom was watching. She was afraid of all kinds of worms, little and big, and snakes fell into the general category. I vowed to come back later to check out the pile on my own. Snakes didn't bother me, just spiders.

From the half-fallen shed, we took out through the field but kept watch for cow patties. The ones we spotted were old and crumbly, but Jerry took a stick to them anyway to see if anything was crawling inside. No luck. We kept walking. Eight acres took time to explore.

"Look at that!" Mom saw them first—clusters of big, black lusciousness. A huge patch of blackberries grew along the fence at the back of our eight acres! Jerry and I started to run. Mom broke into a jog. The patch was even bigger than we first thought and ran both sides of the fence from corner to corner.

"Dessert!" Mom smiled through her first mouthful. We picked and ate until our fingers were purple and our lips bruised with the sweet, black juice. When we were full, the long, leafy canes still bent heavy like we had never picked a one. "We got to get some pans." Mom was thrilled. We set a fast pace to the house and back again, loaded with every pan we could carry.

All afternoon we shuttled back and forth from the patch to the kitchen, and by the end, every bowl and pan and even the sink overflowed. Mom set about cleaning the black beauties and heating sugared batches on the propane stove. I found the box of canning jars we had brought from North Carolina and carefully washed each one. Jerry hauled in water to boil off the germs, and then he dug into boxes looking for the block of paraffin. By five thirty, when Daddy drove up, we had twenty-five jars of blackberry jam lined up on the kitchen table. Mom saved out some of the berries to eat for supper.

"Too bad there wasn't time to make a real dessert," she lamented as Daddy popped a handful of fresh berries into his mouth.

His eyes twinkled with a surprise. "I think I can solve that problem." He began to unload the grocery bag, and when he got to the bottom, he pulled out a separate bag made of extra-heavy paper meant to keep things cold. I thought I knew what it was, but I didn't want to guess in case I was wrong. "Get out some bowls, Eva," he said, "and some spoons, Sweet Potato. We got to eat this now before it melts." So we had cold,

creamy vanilla ice cream and just-picked blackberries for supper on our first real night in the Ohio house. Never did a dessert taste so good. It was a "welcome to Ohio" surprise.

The Driveway Deal

Daddy never met a price he liked. No matter what was selling or who was selling it, Daddy believed that the asking price was just the starting point, and a high one at that. He always wanted to "Jew them down," as he put it. Mom said that was not a nice thing to say about the Jews—Jesus was a Jew after all—but Daddy said the Jews were smart at business and so was he. So he tried to get the price down. It was a game to him, a matter of pride. And even though Mom always warned, "You get what you pay for," it was very important to Daddy to pay the very least amount he could for whatever he bought. That's what made Jerry cry.

Before our first summer in Ohio, we had never lived anyplace where many kids had bikes. Or if we did live where bikes could be fun, we never stayed long enough to get one. Like I said before, we moved a lot.

But after the truck finally arrived from North Carolina with the rest of our furniture, and after the driver and his helper unloaded the davenport and the two gray chairs that matched, and after the big wood table was set by the window in the front room and the heavy wood chairs stood around it waiting for company or Thanksgiving or any occasion special enough to eat someplace besides the kitchen, and after Daddy got the beds from the trailer put up so we all had a decent place to sleep—after all that, life in Ohio began to settle in and feel normal. Mom cooked, ironed, and swept floors. Daddy went to work early and stayed late. Jerry hauled water for the wash tubs, and I carried trash to the burn barrel and emptied the pot.

Emptying the poop pot was a job no one wanted, but neither did anyone want to hike up to the outhouse in the middle of the night. So for emergencies we kept a white metal pot in the curtained closet off the kitchen. I lifted the pot lid every morning, hoping for no nighttime deposits, but if there were, I very carefully carried it up the path to the outhouse—the outhouse with spiders. Did I mention the creepy, beady-eyed spiders?

But aside from hauling water and dumping poop pots, Jerry and I were mostly free to roam the eight acres and beyond. That's how we got to know our neighbors.

Mrs. Murdock was closest. Her house was much smaller than ours, just a kitchen, front room, and bedroom all on

41

one floor, but it sat on a big piece of land, probably around eight acres, same as ours. An old rusty car crumbled on the gravel drive that was all overgrown with grass and weeds. The grown-over car looked like someone had driven it in, parked, and then had never come back to drive it out. Maybe that's just what Mr. Murdock had done: drove in from work, died in his bed in the middle of the night, and never got up to drive out again.

When Mrs. Murdock mentioned the car and her plan to have it towed away, she called it "The Machine," not "automobile" or "car" like most people. Daddy said that *machine* was an old-time word for *car*, and Mrs. Murdock was very old, so I guess it fit. Her dog, Buster, was old too—and gray and slow just like Mrs. Murdock. Buster was tied out back of Mrs. Murdock's house, and he barked and barked and barked. He wanted to be loose, but he never got his wish as far as I know. Every day Mrs. Murdock fixed Buster a dog pancake made up of table scraps and beat-up eggs all fried together. It smelled bad, but Buster liked it and stopped barking long enough to wolf it down. The pancakes must have been good for him, because he kept going. Maybe Mr. Murdock could have used one of those pancakes.

Mom and Mrs. Murdock talked across the fence sometimes and admired each other's flowers. Mom planted hollyhocks that bloomed creamy white and looked like flared skirts for dancing girls. Mrs. Murdock had pink sweet peas that twirled their vines in and out of the fence wires. Sometimes, when Mrs. Murdock was outside, she invited me to crawl through the fence hole and visit in her yard. We talked about birds but mostly about her cherry tree that was full of sour pie cherries every June. "Maybe your mom will make a pie," she offered. Sounded good to me.

The Whittles lived on our other side, across from where the garden would be next summer. We didn't see the Whittles much. Mom said they weren't very neighborly, but that was just how some folks were, so we were to leave them alone. And I would have, except for Edith. She was the Whittles' daughter and my age or thereabouts. The first week we lived on Leap Road I saw Edith outside, so I walked across the not-yet garden to say hi.

"Wanna come over and play?" I offered in my friend-liest voice.

"I'm not allowed out of the yard," she almost whispered. Her toes were lined up, twitching, at the edge of the not-yet garden.

"Okay, well, I can come over there." I stepped over the edge onto the Whittles' grass.

"You're not allowed in my yard," she spoke quickly and glanced over her shoulder. I was surprised by a hint of alarm in her voice. I stepped back from the grass onto our not-yet garden.

"Then how're we gonna play if you can't come over here

43

and I can't go over there?" I was perplexed.

"We can't play." Edith turned away, back to her house. That was all I saw of Edith until the Weed Tea Party. And that's a story I definitely wrote down in my yellow tablet.

Claris Anne Sparks lived on the other side of the Whittles, and her mother made dresses out of fifty-pound feed sacks—and aprons, too, from the leftover pieces. Mr. Sparks worked at a flour mill and he brought home stacks of the printed cloth sacks.

"Mr. Sparks has got a good eye for the purdy ones," Mrs. Sparks told me the first time she showed off the stack of feed sacks by her sewing machine. I agreed. The sacks that he selected were bright with color—lots of pink and blue flowers with the occasional reds and purples mixed in and sometimes twisty green vines along the sides. They sewed up really nice. You'd never believe they started as wheat bags, but Mrs. Sparks didn't care even if you did know.

"I just thank the Lord that I can take something low and make it into something high." Mrs. Sparks talked in churchy words. "It's like Jesus preached in the Bible," she went on. "The high will be brought low and the low will be lifted up." I didn't know much about the Bible, but the feed sack dresses looked nice.

The Sparks family was really friendly, and even though Claris Anne was older than me, she still invited me to play sometimes. She knew how to twirl a baton, and she had one made of a metal rod with sparkling ends. She could twirl fast with either hand, pass the baton behind her back, and even throw it up high, catch it, and never miss a twirl. She practiced a lot so she could be a majorette. I liked that she let me have a turn even though it was her baton and I wasn't good at all.

One afternoon between twirls, I told Claris Anne about Edith and what happened that day at the edge of the not-yet garden, but she said to pay no attention to Edith's ways. "It's her family, not her."

The Grays up the road had lots of kids, mostly boys, except Margie, who was out of high school and studying to be a nurse, and another girl who was still so little I didn't know her name. Everyone just called her The Baby. It was the Gray boys who got Jerry all riled up to have a bike of his own.

Allen and Mike Gray rode their bikes everywhere and all the time, up and down Leap Road. They passed our house twenty or more times a day. Often they stopped to talk to Jerry in the yard, and sometimes the three of them waded in the ditch in front and crawled through the culvert pipe that ran under our drive. Other times they parked their bikes and all three boys took out through the back field and stayed all afternoon. I wasn't invited, so I don't know what they did back there, though I figured they maybe smoked because I could smell cigarette stink on Jerry's clothes when he came in.

But sometimes the Gray boys just wanted to ride their

bikes. They did tricks on them like no-hands steering and "the bucking horse," where they'd hoist the front wheel in the air and ride on the back tire, or—the best—get up speed and stand on the seat with their arms flung out like they were flying. The Gray boys could do good bike tricks.

Some days they skipped the tricks and just raced to see who was fastest. They'd start in front of their drive and peddle like crazy past our house and on to the finish line at the end of the Mere's drive. The Mere's place was quite a piece past Mrs. Murdock's on the other side of a pasture. Jerry wanted to join the fun, and he would be the starter sometimes or the finish line judge, but never a racer, which was what he longed to be. To be a racer you had to have a bike of your own.

So Jerry started a campaign to get Daddy to buy him a bike, and he knew exactly the one he had to have. It was a red Schwinn with a tank and a headlight in front and a long passenger seat over the back fender. The Sears catalog had a picture of it on page 304 with the $59.95 price printed underneath the description. Jerry just about wore out the paper looking at that picture. He carried the catalog around with him, rolled up with a rubber band, and he'd tell anyone who would listen all about the Schwinn. It was a good-looking bike, no doubt. I knew Mike and Allen would be jealous (probably part of the point) if Jerry got it—which seemed as likely as a "snowball's chance," as Grandpa would say. We all knew the ending to that was "in hell," but Grandma scowled if he added it. No matter—we got the meaning. Jerry's Schwinn bike dreams would surely melt away to nothing.

But Donnie Boggs was selling a bike. The sign on the road said so. The Boggs family lived in a beat-down place on Leap just the other side of Jeanette Road. The Gray boys saw the sign on one of their rides and raced to tell Jerry. The sign said to come after 6:00 p.m., so Jerry camped out at the end of our drive to wait for Daddy to get home.

"Hold on, son." Daddy waved him off. "Let me get out of the car, and then you can tell me." Jerry spilled it all out in his firecracker bursts of energy—the bike for sale, the after-six part, how it was past that already, and how they just had to get down to the Boggs' house now or the bike would surely be gone. "After supper, Jerry. After supper will be soon enough." Daddy's weary reply was the opposite of Jerry's fireworks. Jerry was crazy disappointed by the wait, but there was nothing to be done about it. They would go when Daddy was ready.

It wasn't my business, but I climbed into the Dodge anyway when Daddy and Jerry headed out for the short ride up the road to the Boggs' place. We pulled all the way up the drive and Daddy and Jerry got out. Mr. Boggs and Donnie had their heads deep inside the hood of an old car. After Mr. Boggs wiped his greasy fingers on a rag, he offered a hand to Daddy. Donnie went around the back of the house to pull out the bike for inspection. It was kind of like the catalog picture, but old, with chips out of the red-and-white paint on the tank. The chrome handlebars had some rust spots, and the headlamp didn't light when Jerry tried it. "All 't needs is new batteries." Donnie scuffed his bare foot in the dry dirt. "Wanna take a ride?" he finished.

Jerry climbed on and rode down the dusty drive, came back, and gave it a spin around the house over the patches of weeds and rocks. I was surprised at how good he could ride. He hadn't had much practice. After a couple more trips, he pulled up in front of Donnie. "Rides pretty good," he said. Donnie nodded. "Why're you sellin' it?" A fair question.

"Not much time for bikes no more." Donnie looked down. "Helpin' my dad with ta' cars." He pointed his chin toward the old car where his head had been hiding. Donnie was older than us by several years, and Claris Anne said he didn't go to school much anymore. Guess his dad thought he could learn more useful things under a car hood than at school.

Jerry liked the bike; it was plain on his face. Daddy knew it too. I saw him glancing Jerry's way. But Daddy and Mr. Boggs were still standing stiff by the old car—talking, but not comfortable. From my backseat view, I couldn't tell why. Lots of times I didn't understand grown-ups and how they acted around each other. It was like they spoke a secret language. But I did hear Daddy say, "What'd ya asking for the bike?"

"Donnie's business. His bike." Mr. Boggs was short and clear. Daddy turned to Donnie.

"What'd ya asking, son?"

Donnie studied his dusty feet. "Twenty" was all he said.

"Too much," Daddy came back. "I'll give you ten." Jerry's face flared red, and then his chin dropped toward his chest.

"No." Donnie held firm. "Twenty."

"Let's go, Jerry." Daddy turned and started to our car. Jerry pleaded with his eyes and didn't move. "I said let's go," Daddy answered.

It happened fast. We were all back in the Dodge—Jerry and Daddy in front as before, and I was still in the back. Daddy pushed his foot down on the starter, hit the clutch to shift into reverse, and the car started its roll backward out of the drive. My eyes were on Jerry. I had never seen him like that. He was bawling like an orphaned calf. Tears, rage, disappointment, humiliation all showed on his face. "Please! Please! Please!" was all he could say. But Daddy never looked his way, just watched the mirror as we backed down the long drive.

We were about to pull onto Leap Road and head home when I spotted Donnie. He was galloping down the drive after us. "Wait!" he yelled over and over. Daddy rolled down the window when Donnie caught up to the car. "I'll take ten." Daddy put the car in first and we pulled back to the house to make the deal. Daddy slid his wallet from his hip. He handed Donnie a ten-dollar bill, we loaded Jerry's new bike, and we left for home.

Daddy was proud that he got a "good deal" and kept repeating that Jerry learned an important lesson that day. Jerry got his bike, that was true, but I was not sure he learned the lesson Daddy thought. The whole thing made me sad, and maybe it made Jerry sad too. I don't know. For him it may have been enough just to get the bike. That night I wrote it all down in my story tablet to see if I could figure things out.

The Paint Job

Aunt Alice was coming! Mom got a letter that said so. She was coming on the train to Union Station in downtown Columbus and would be at our house on August 10 to stay for a week. I hadn't seen Mom smile so much for a long time, maybe ever. But as she began to think about things, the smile faded. "I wish this place was better" was all she said. And for the first time, I knew that Mom was ashamed of where we lived.

I wasn't sure exactly why the shame—the house seemed okay to me. Maybe it was the outhouse and having to haul water from the outside spigot that bothered her. I was used to both by then and didn't think anything about it anymore. But Mom's sister Alice was a city girl. Maybe that was the real problem in Mom's mind.

Alice was the youngest of the Johnson Clan—the unlucky thirteenth. It seemed, though, that things had worked out okay for her despite the bad number. Education was a big part of her good luck. Uncle Walter, Johnson Clan number eleven, went to college on the GI Bill (which meant the government paid for his education because he was a soldier), but Alice and Mable, who was a teacher, were the only Johnson girls out of ten who got to go on in school. Mom started high school but never finished, a decision she regretted, she told me over and over. "You got more chances, Carol. Don't be like me. Finish school," Mom advised me, "so you can amount to something."

I guess Alice had "amounted to something" in Mom's eyes because she had graduated from high school and gone on to secretarial college. She had a good job, Mom said, typing and taking dictation in her spiral notebook at the Naval Academy in Annapolis, Maryland. Alice dressed fancy for her job: high-heeled shoes like stilts and hair all done up. I had seen the pictures she'd sent Mom in a card. I was sure she had a water spigot that worked and a bathroom in her house.

So Mom was worried that our place wasn't good enough, and I could see she was figuring things. By the time Daddy got home, she had a plan. "Ross, there's nothing to be done about the outhouse, but we got to at least get the water line into the kitchen before Alice gets here." Daddy knew not to argue.

"I'm not working Sunday," he offered. "I'll dig the trench to lay the pipe then. It'll take all day." Daddy hardly ever had Sunday off. He worked seven days most weeks. "Can't turn down the money." He'd shrug. "It's time and a half pay on Saturday and double time on Sunday." On his first day off in weeks, he would still work all day. But there was nothing to do, but to do.

Mom wouldn't dig, but she would paint—every wall in the house. She had her plan, as I said. Mom had wanted to paint ever since we stepped into the Ohio house, and even I could see why. Every wall that wasn't bare brick was made of flattened-out pasteboard boxes taped together and nailed to wood studs. Some of the cardboard walls were just plain brown, but most were printed all over with pictures that showed what the boxes had held. We had Campbell's Tomato Juice walls in the front room, Del Monte Cling Peaches in the kitchen, and even Rolling Rock Beer in the bedroom. Like I said, we needed to paint. With Daddy working steady and extra, we could buy what we needed to do the job. And Aunt Alice's visit had put the speed on things.

Mom studied the paint chart from the hardware store and decided on colors—forest green for the front room, sunshine yellow in the kitchen to brighten it up, cloud blue for Mom and Daddy's bedroom downstairs, and apple blossom for the whole upstairs, including Jerry's bedroom and mine. I was okay with apple blossom. Jerry would have preferred something besides pink, and said so, but that was Mom's decision.

The project began. On Monday, Mom raised her step-ladder and started in the soon-to-be-green front room. She filled the paint pan and started rolling. It went pretty fast except for the trim close to the ceiling and the floor—both were bare wood and hard to clean up if the paint dripped or smeared, but Mom was a careful painter. Soon the Campbell's Tomato Juice ad was covered over along with all the others. By suppertime, the entire front room was transformed to forest green from top to bottom. And so it continued on Tuesday, Wednesday, and Thursday. By Friday, Mom had just the apple-blossom upstairs to paint. She was tired but determined. Jerry and I helped as best we could by staying out of her way and by making our own toast breakfast and peanut butter sandwich lunches. Mom had a pot of pintos on the stove for supper when Daddy got home, and he didn't complain about eating beans every day. He filled up on bread and buttermilk if they weren't enough for him.

Sunday we rested. The painting was done, and we all admired how different the rooms looked. The water line was in, too, because Daddy had dug a little every night instead of leaving it to the weekend. Water from the kitchen spigot was a little miracle. We had just last-minute details to finish— Mom opened all the windows to get rid of the paint smell, and Jerry got ready to sleep on the davenport in the front room because Aunt Alice would have his bed while she visited. He had a double bed, so it made the most sense.

Monday came and dragged on forever as we waited. Mom planned baked chicken for supper and had the drumsticks and other pieces buttered, floured, and laid out on the cookie sheet. It wouldn't go in the oven until five thirty so it would come out sizzling hot for supper.

"Shuck the corn, Carol." Mom pointed me to the dozen ears soaking in a bucket. Since our not-yet garden was not yet until next summer, Daddy had to buy the corn at a roadside stand. I lifted the corn bucket and headed outside. Every silky hair would be gone from the ears before I brought them back. I was the best shucker, Mom said.

Mom sent Jerry down the road to the Cantrells' house to buy eggs. They kept chickens in their back field—a rooster that puffed up big and shiny when he crowed and about a dozen hens that pecked and scratched all day around their chicken house. The Cantrells didn't sell their hens to eat, but they did sell fresh eggs if they had extras. Sometimes the eggs were still warm from the nest if you went early in the morning just after Mrs. Cantrell collected them from under the hens. We always got eggs from the Cantrells if we could.

The eggs were for breakfast while Aunt Alice visited, and for supper corn bread to go with the chicken. Mom had the iron skillet out and the cornmeal and buttermilk beside the mixing bowl. When she was ready, she'd plop a big glob of bacon grease into the skillet and heat the oven with the skillet inside. It would be smoking hot when she poured in the batter. "That's what makes a good crust," Mom said, and she was so right. I could almost taste the finished bread—soft and creamy yellow on the inside and crunchy crisp all over the outside. There was not much better than Mom's corn bread.

The time ticked, and finally there was nothing left to do but wait. Mom fussed around the front room, Jerry fired off to ride bikes with the Gray boys, and I tried to read a book about Wild Bill Hickok and Calamity Jane. I loved stories about cowboys and Wild West stuff. Books about Wild Bill and Calamity usually were hard to put down, but that day my attention was on the front window instead of on cattle rustling and shoot-outs. Ticktock.

And then the yellow cab was there! Mom rushed out and so did I. The driver opened the back door for Aunt Alice and then turned to the taxi trunk to unload her suitcase. I should say *suitcases* because there were three of them. One was a monster, one a medium size, and the third a square box of a thing with a handle on top. Mom took that, the overnight case, she called it. She put it down with the other cases we had hauled in and lined up on the bare-wood front-room floor. They all matched up like a family wearing the same outfit. I never knew suitcases could match. I guess that's how folks did things in Annapolis where Aunt Alice lived.

Mom fluttered and smiled. Aunt Alice did too. They were best girlfriends who hadn't seen each other for a long time. And that was the way the week-long visit went. They were both full of stories and memories of their growing-up time in the "hollers" of West Virginia. They talked about Poppy's "Johnson Eye," and about Mommy taking off on the train "at every whipstitch" to help whoever in the family had a new baby. Mom told her best story again about how she had "wailed the tar outta Virginia" that time her sister had worn Mom's best dress to school without asking.

"I waited for her in the outhouse," Mom started, "and when I saw her comin' down the path, I jumped out and started beatin' on her. Mommy had to pull me off." Mom had been a scrapper as a girl, and she could hardly talk from laughing so much at the memory. "She never took my clothes again after that. Afraid to," Mom finished with a smile. Aunt Alice doubled over laughing and hooted like a barn owl, which she always did when she was really tickled. Her hoots made me laugh just to hear them. The sisters stayed up late every night, and I could hear them talking—sometimes in low, serious voices and sometimes giggling like girls.

Turned out that Aunt Alice didn't care about the outhouse or the bare floors or any of the other things Mom worried about. She was just as glad to be with Mom as Mom was to be with her. Mom was different around her sister. She laughed a lot and talked, talked, talked like she'd been saving up for a long time. I realized how lonely Mom was in "middle-of-nowhere Hilliard, Ohio," as she told Aunt Alice. I hadn't known that before. I just thought it was Mom's way to be really quiet and act like a dark shadow was on her all the time. Until Aunt Alice came for a visit, I didn't know Mom could be happy.

But the happiness left with Aunt Alice, and Mom was even quieter and darker than before. She always worked hard, but after Aunt Alice was gone, Mom started working like crazy.

On Mondays she washed our clothes by hand in the washer tub and pushed them through the wringer to rinse and wring again. She hung Daddy's blue work pants on the lines, along with Jerry's jeans and my denim overalls. By evening they were dry. After supper she sprinkled each piece with water and rolled them to dampen, so that on Tuesdays she could iron all day. On Wednesdays she swept and mopped and dusted. On Thursdays she canned green beans, tomatoes, or whatever vegetable or fruit Daddy brought in from the roadside stand. On Fridays she embroidered flowers on stacks of pillowcases and tablecloths. When Mom was in her work frenzy after Aunt Alice went back to Annapolis, even Saturdays and Sundays were busy days. It seemed Mom never stopped. Maybe she worked to keep the sad away.

Weed Tea

I didn't have too much time to think about Mom and her working because I had my own worries. I was going to a new school, and I was both excited and scared. I really liked school, and I was smart (a personal opinion I never said out loud). I got As in everything. But what if I was behind in my work because we moved a lot before getting to Hilliard? What if nobody liked me at the new school? What if Ohio teachers were mean?

Claris Anne had lots of experience at the Hilliard School. When I asked, she told me all about the building—which was new and still smelled fresh—and about what it was like to ride the bus: "Try for a seat near the driver because the troublemakers sit in the back." She also warned me against Miss Martin, the meanest teacher. "Just hope you don't get her," Claris Anne advised, "or it'll be a long, hard year for sure." I thought I could get a front bus seat because Leap Road was near the beginning of the bus route, but I didn't see that there was anything I could do to get around the Miss Martin possibility except hope for the best and worry the worst could happen anyway. On the first day of school, I would find out who my teacher was, and not before.

I appreciated all Claris Anne tried to do to prepare me, but she was several grades ahead, and I feared her information might be out of date. The person I really wanted to talk to about school was Edith. She was my age and my grade and would be most likely to have the real scoop about how to act and what to look out for. But Edith had already decided that I was one of the people she would avoid, so getting the school rundown from her seemed unlikely. I hadn't seen her in weeks—not even from a distance on my way to the outhouse. Unlike us, the Whittles had a bathroom inside. Their cars (they had two because Mrs. Whittle could drive!) came and went every day. Mr. Whittle mowed the grass on Saturday unless it rained, and on Monday morning Mrs. Whittle hung clothes on the line in the backyard—again, unless it rained. Other than that, it was almost like the Whittle family didn't live next door, or if they did live there, they didn't have any kids. I had no idea what Edith did all day.

But I really wanted to ask her about school. I considered the direct approach: march over to her house and knock until someone answered, preferably Edith. Maybe she couldn't turn me down if I just showed up. But she might. Or worse, her mother, who was just as mysterious as Edith, might open the door, or her father who never waved. I kept thinking on the problem for several days. No solution came, and I finally gave up the idea of the school talk. But then Edith surprised me.

It was a drippy, hot day in late August—one of those days when you could hardly bear to move and when no drink was cold enough to cool you down. I almost wanted to climb inside the icebox and lie like a big ham next to the ice chunk that Daddy had hauled in from the store. I rejected the icebox (a bad idea for lots of reasons, including the possibility that I could get locked inside) and gave in to the heat.

If I was going to be sweaty no matter what I did, I might as well go do what I liked best. I headed to the back field for a walk. I never knew what I would find there, but it was almost always interesting and different every time. I headed past the slag pile where the coal pile would be come winter, past the spider outhouse, the burn barrel, and the falling-down shed where there might be snakes, though I hadn't found any yet. On the way to the field I teetered again on top of the piled wood because I knew Mom was resting on the davenport trying to stay cool and wouldn't know to stop me—the worm thing, you know. But it was too hot even for snakes to sun themselves, so I moved into the knee-high grass along the fence next to Mrs. Murdock's. I followed it back to the shallow creek bed on the other side of the blackberry bushes that marked the end of our acres.

I considered climbing over the fence and into the next field but decided against it. I didn't know who owned it—someone who lived on Jeanette Road, we thought—and sometimes we could hear rifle shots coming from over that way. It was just target practice probably, but best to stay away. Daddy had said a rifle shot could travel a mile or more.

The creek was not much on its best day and completely dry most of the time, so I wasn't surprised to find it was parched and cracked by the heat. But the grasshoppers were all around to put on a show, rising up in unexpected spurts to hop or fly from plant to plant. They were just the color of the brown-tinged weeds of late summer and very hard to detect unless they moved. I was patient and watchful until I caught one in my cupped hand. I gazed into its bulgy eyes and inspected its scaly body and hinged back legs that made it such a good hopper. It spit brown tobacco juice on my fingers until I let it go. As the grasshopper took off to do its important bug business, I spotted a monarch butterfly. The field was full of milkweed, which made a good hunting ground for monarchs because milkweed was their favorite. I liked milkweed, too, but for a different reason. A ripe, burst-open milkweed pod looked like a brown fish with seed "scales" that flew in all directions in the wind.

I didn't find any pods that were ready to fly, so I followed the dry creek to the place where the fence joined the one going back to the house—the stretch of wire that separated our acres from the Whittles' property. It was a good place to pick Queen Anne's lace and some goldenrod that was just showing its late-August yellow. Mom would put them in a vase on the big table. I watched out for the bees that were drawn to the hot-blossom sweetness and buzzed from flower to flower to suck up the nectar. Like the bees, I roamed haphazardly from cluster to cluster, snapping the stems and arranging the bouquet in my free hand.

"Those are really pretty." I jumped, totally surprised by the voice. Edith was standing just on the other side of the fence. She could have been there all the time I was collecting flowers, but I was so focused on avoiding bees and finding the fullest blooms that I didn't notice her.

"Thanks," I said. "I think so too." I kept it short for fear I would scare her off with too many words. "Want me to pick you some?"

"I have my own, but not many goldenrods." She held up her own bouquet.

"I have lots," I offered, "and Queen Anne's lace. Do you want a few of those too?" I handed some of my goldenrod and white, lacy Queen Anne through the fence.

"Don't you have any of the purple ones like these?" She pointed to the ironweed in her bouquet. "We can share." Edith passed some of the purple clusters through the fence, and they were a great addition to my collection.

That's how we began. We walked along side by side, the fence between us, picking flowers and sharing back and forth. We talked about how pretty the bouquets were and how hot it was and how summer was ending, and then we talked about school. Edith warned me about the Triple M— Mean Miss Martin. She even demonstrated how Miss Martin would stand with her arms crossed and a frown so mean you could feel it all the way to the end of the hall. We both laughed at that. She said Connie was really nice and could be a good friend and that she'd heard about a new girl named Thelma who wore dungarees and overalls all the time, which the teachers wouldn't like. Only dresses were proper for girls, they said. "So stay clear of Thelma," Edith advised.

Edith went on to admire Carla's jump-rope skills. "She can do all kinds of special jump tricks—Double Dutch even. And in jacks, Pat can go all the way to tens and back down and never miss."

She explained that girls couldn't climb to the top on the jungle bars because some boys liked to get under and look up our dresses. (I already knew that, but I didn't say so.) And I was really happy to hear that jumping out of the swings was allowed. I loved to pump so high I could look over the top bar and then bail out on the downswing.

Miss Roberts was the music teacher, and Mr. Moore was the principal, who smiled a lot but could be strict, according to Edith. Mrs. Shaw was the best teacher to hope for. Miss Trasfer was all right, but not as good as Mrs. Shaw. And so the fence talk went . . . until we got to the outbuilding.

The Whittles' outbuilding was an empty shed that stood next to the fence within sight of their house, but it was mostly hidden by some overgrown evergreens. We stopped before we could be seen. Then, "Do you want to come for tea?" Edith pointed to a hole in the wire where I could slip through. Without another word, I put one leg through and then slid my head, body, and other leg over the line onto the Whittles' side of the field. Edith opened the shed door, and we went inside without a word.

The shed was not empty, as I thought it would be, or filled with dusty junk. There was a round wooden table in the middle with chairs all around. Curtains hung at the window, and cups and saucers lined the side shelves. Four spoons were carefully laid next to them on white embroidered napkins. The uppermost shelf had two pans with lids and a metal teapot. This was a miniature house, a playhouse, not an abandoned shed.

"We can make some Weed Tea," Edith offered as she pulled one pan and the teapot from the shelf. "Would you get the cups and saucers?" she directed me. And so began our Weed Tea Party.

All that hot afternoon we spent making tea of various kinds—goldenrod tea, elm leaf tea, plantain tea, grass tea (really bad), and of course, dandelion (the second best) and mint from a wild patch that grew next to the shed. Mint tea took first place. We lifted our cups with a thumb and one finger while daintily holding out a pinky. We talked with an accent and giggled and pretended we were fine ladies from England where tea parties were an every day event.

As dusk cooled and settled the hot day, the shadows finally overtook us. I went home with the first lightning bugs and got to the kitchen door just as Mom was calling us in for supper.

Daddy was full of news about the United Auto Workers (UAW) union at the Columbus Auto Parts (the shop) where he worked. There was serious talk, he told us, about going out on strike to get higher pay and some other things that were better for the workers.

"But," Daddy hit his fist on the table, "the #&*! Republicans in Washington are doing everything they can to break the union and keep workers from getting what we deserve." Daddy's language always got "colorful," Mom said, when he talked about the Republicans. They really got him worked up. "They're always trying to take food out of the mouth of the Working Man." Daddy meant himself, us, our family.

Mom gave Daddy a look that meant he should watch his language, but there was no stopping him. "Republicans in Washington put through that Taft-Hartley Act—" (more swearing—lots of it). Daddy didn't glance at Mom. "Lied about it all the way. Said it was a 'Right to Work' law. What it is, is the 'Right to Scab!' Made it legal for plant owners to bring in scab workers to steal our jobs! That's what Taft-Hartley does!"

Talking about Scabs got Daddy red-in-the-face mad. Scabs were workers from outside who didn't belong to the union. They would work for less money, so the company hired them to take the striking workers' jobs and break the union's strike.

"President Truman tried to fight it," Daddy raged on about Taft-Hartley, "but the Republicans and some of the turncoat Blue Dog Democrats rammed it through." Daddy slammed his fist on the table again. "Never would have happened under Roosevelt," Daddy finished. "He took up for workers and their families."

Daddy was union through and through and a hard-core Democrat. Mom had always been both, but that wasn't true for Daddy. "Used to be a Republican, was raised that way," he often said, "but Herbert Hoover was the last Republican I ever voted for or ever will." Daddy, and a lot of people, blamed the Depression on President Hoover. I didn't know about that, but I did know that the Depression had been really hard times for Mom and Daddy and most all the people in the United States.

"Nobody could find a job because there weren't any to find," Daddy always said when he got to talking about the

Depression. "Nobody had money. People had to stand in line just to get a loaf a' bread to have something to put in their stomachs. We had to scrape even to have enough to buy milk for Norma when she was a baby."

"But we always managed to do that at least," Mom put in, "even if your daddy and I didn't have anything to eat." Mom was both proud and sad at the memory.

"Your daddy took any little job he could get. I took in laundry," she went on, "just to get a little money in the house. Washed work clothes for a baker. He had one of the few steady jobs around. Guess people need bread no matter how bad the times are." Mom paused. "Oh my land, those white pants of his were so hard to get clean. Full of flour and short-ening. Had to boil 'em on the stove, scrub 'em with a brush, and wring 'em by hand. And then they had to be ironed just so." Mom shook her head. "Baker paid me a dollar a week to do his clothes. Wasn't hardly anything, but we were glad to get it. Cash money was hard to come by, and so was food. Was many a time greens out of the garden was the only thing we had to eat for supper. Didn't even have money to buy a little piece of salt pork to put in 'em for flavor."

I understood why Daddy and Mom were strong on the union and on the Democrats. That's who had their back in hard times—not the rich people with powerful jobs who ran everything, and not the Republicans who "just looked out for the Rockefellers," as Daddy said.

"We'd never have made it if it hadn't been for FDR," Mom said. "President Roosevelt got this country through the Depression and got us back to work. He saved us all," she finished. Franklin Roosevelt was a Democrat, and the people just kept reelecting him to be president. "I cried like a baby when he died. It was just too sad," Mom finished the memory.

We spent so much time on the union news and on politics and the Depression memories that I never got around to telling about Edith and the Weed Tea Party. But that was okay because I liked the union news and the politics. I felt important to be included in the grown-ups' talk. Besides, I thought I finally had found a real Ohio friend in Edith, and that was enough. Unfortunately, things didn't work out the way I hoped.

Day One

I didn't see Edith the next day or the next or the next, even though I went back to the field and walked the fence line to the outbuilding several times over the last days of summer. I finally resigned to wait for the first day of school. I would surely see her on the school bus, and maybe even get to sit with her on the ride.

At eight on the Tuesday morning after Labor Day, Jerry and I stood waiting by our vulture-like mailbox at the end of the driveway. Breakfast eggs sat warm in our stomachs, and we both had a dollar—our lunch money for the week. Mrs. Sparks had passed on the information about the lunch price. "The homeroom teacher will collect it," she said, "first thing in the morning. The kids can pack if you'd rather, but Claris Anne says the hot lunch in the cafeteria is pretty good most days." The Gray boys confirmed the "pretty good" part of the advice, so we had our hot-lunch dollar.

I also had fresh #2 pencils that stuck out like yellow ears in the flap of the ringed notebook I cradled in my right arm. I'd probably need a few other school supplies, but I'd wait for the list from my teacher—whoever that turned out to be. Mrs. Shaw, I hoped.

The school bus route traveled north on Leap toward Cemetery Road, then on for several miles and turns to the school building on Main Street in town. Leap Road was lined up and down with other kids—the Grays, the Mere kids, Claris Anne, and even the Mitchel tribe, almost out of sight at the end of the road by the railroad crossing. They would be the first of the Leap Road kids to board. The Mitchels didn't venture down our way very often, and I had been to their house only once, so I didn't know them very well at all. In fact, I was surprised to see how many were standing by the roadside for the bus. There were at least five, and maybe six, but I couldn't quite tell from the distance.

Leap Road families didn't have much (except maybe the Whittles), but the Mitchels had the least of us all. Even I could tell that their clothes were patched and worn more than the rest of us, and all summer I never saw a Mitchel in shoes. I guess shoes were just for school. I was there at lunchtime the one day I played at their house and discovered that eating was a random affair for the Mitchel family. Kids wandered into the kitchen whenever they got hungry and helped themselves to a bowl of oatmeal. That was all there was to eat, just oatmeal. No milk to pour on top, no raisins, no toast or jam. Just oatmeal—leftover oatmeal that sat cold and sticky in a big pot on the back of the stove. A lot of flies buzzed around the pot and the table. Mom would have gotten the fly swatter and killed every last one if it had been our kitchen, but none of the Mitchels seemed bothered. Guess they were used to having no screens on the doors. Other than the flies and the mushy, cold oatmeal, the Mitchel kids seemed nice enough, but they mostly kept to themselves.

I heard the school bus before I saw it. It inched like an orange caterpillar around the curve by the railroad crossing and stopped to gobble up the Mitchel kids. It rumbled and gobbled from stop to stop—the Grays, some older kids I didn't know, Claris Anne, and then on to the Whittles. But in a mild panic I realized that Edith was not by her mailbox. She was going to miss the bus on the very first day! Where was she?

And then I saw her.

The Whittles' second car, the Nash, the one Mrs. Whittle drove, came floating out of their drive. The "machine" oiled past us without even a wave from the driver or the passenger. Edith slumped down in the front seat and looked only at the road in front of her. She would not ride the school bus that day or any other. Her mother always drove her to school.

I trailed the Nash with my eyes until it was out of sight.

By then the bus had stopped for us, and Jerry fired up the steps like he always did. He headed down the aisle to the back where Allen and Mike Gray sat two across on the slick brown seat. They scrunched tighter so Jerry could join them. Since Edith was a no-show, I took my time getting on while my mind worked out a new seating plan for myself. I spotted Claris Anne, who waved encouragement, but she was already sitting with an older girl I didn't know, so I settled into a seat by myself and slid over to the window. I wasn't sure I wanted some strange kid to sit beside me, but I left the aisle seat open just in case. I could make a friend, but then again the kid might be weird. You never knew.

The place next to me stayed empty as kids who got on passed by to sit with friends they hadn't seen all summer. I looked out the window with an I-don't-care stare pasted on my face. As the trip went on, the other seats filled, and the empty seat beside me began to "stick out like a sore thumb," as Grandpa would say. I began to smell the cootie stink—on me—and it was just my first day at the Ohio school. The bus rumbled on.

At the edge of town, the orange bus-worm stopped to gobble up the last rider. The driver flung open the door in front of a bare-block garage house. It was even smaller than Mrs. Murdock's, but it did have a front porch, which I noticed right away. The garage house sat so close to the road that there was no yard to speak of. A girl waited on the dusty strip, and even from the bus window, I could see she was different. The dungarees made her stand out—not a single other girl had on dungarees—but that wasn't what I had noticed, or the red plaid shirt. It was the calm and the confidence that surrounded her even as she stood on the gritty roadside in front of the sad little cinder block building. She wasn't dressed "right," but it didn't matter somehow. She moved down the bus aisle and slid into the seat beside me just like she knew I'd saved it just for her. "Hi, my name's Thelma Rigsby." She lifted her hand in a little wave and then settled in.

As it turned out, I liked Thelma from the start. She was funny and smart, and I saw first off that she went her own way no matter what. Over the school year, I made friends with Connie and Carla and some others, but Thelma and I became best friends. We'd slide double and laugh all the way from the top of the sliding board to the end. Then we'd split at the bottom—Thelma went right and I went left—and race to the ladder again to see who would be first up. And she could get her swing even higher than I could and bail fearlessly onto the playground gravel. A skinned knee was nothing to her. Thelma knew lots of fancy jump-rope moves, which she taught me, and she hardly ever missed in jacks. She'd toss the ball just high enough to scoop up the right number in time to catch the ball on the way down. On the playground, I was better than Thelma at only two things—running and softball. In late spring, my two best skills would come together and cause Mr. Moore to gasp, but that's a story for later.

It was our first day at Hilliard School—and it was *our* first day because Thelma had just moved to Ohio from Kentucky. "I guess I'm a hillbilly," she shared on the bus ride. "My daddy an' granddaddy an' great granddaddy been digging coal outta them hills forever." She was wistful—like me— missing the mountains. "My daddy's got sick from ta' coal an' cain't dig no more. Coughs a lot. Was killin' him, Ma said. We moved. Ma's got people in Columbus that knows about a job." That said it all.

So when the bus bumped to its final stop in front of the school building, we clasped hands and went together to find out our teacher fate. Thelma also knew about the dreaded Triple M—Mean Miss Martin.

As we filed into the building, teachers directed us up the wide center stairs to the auditorium for "the assembly." The auditorium was also the lunchroom, but for the first morning the wooden lunch tables were pushed to the perimeter and the benches were lined together in rows that faced the curtained stage. Flags hung like limp rags on either side of the podium, where a dark-haired man—Mr. Moore, the principal, I guessed—stood waiting for the first-day-back chatter and excitement to quiet. "Good morning," he finally spoke. "Please stand for the pledge."

Shuffle, shuffle . . . hands over hearts: "I pledge allegiance to . . ." And so began my first day at Hilliard School.

After welcomes and introductions, the teachers stood one by one to read the names of kids in their classes. Thelma and I held our breath as one when Miss Martin stood with list in hand. "Mary Ancie." A blonde-haired girl in our row dropped her head. "Mike Baker . . ." And so it went through the alphabet to the Rs. "Don Rager . . . Judy Stevenson . . ." We had escaped! Miss Martin's list skipped right over Richardson and Rigsby! Thelma and I didn't know our teacher's name yet, but we knew it wasn't the Triple M.

The best happened. Thelma and I both got Mrs. Shaw—the teacher prize—and better, we got desks next to each other because Mrs. Shaw seated the class in alphabetical order. I knew then that it was going to be a totally good year . . . until Halloween came, and that kind of messed things up, but that's also a story for later.

The Ginny Window

"Welcome to Room Eleven, kiddos." Mrs. Shaw beamed just outside the classroom on that first day. Twenty of us had followed her out of the auditorium, down the main steps, around the corner, and down more steps so narrow we went single file, and finally we had arrived at the room that would be our school home for the next nine months.

"Welcome, welcome," Mrs. Shaw said again as her gentle hand began to guide each of us through the doorway. "Oh, Ellen, how is your mom?" Mrs. S. leaned close to a dark-haired girl who was first in line. They had a quick, private conversation that left them both with smiles. Ellen disappeared into Room Eleven, and Mrs. Shaw turned her attention to the next in line.

"That must have hurt, Donnie." A tall boy grinned at

the long red scrape that started at his elbow, went down to his wrist, and ended in a scarlet squirt on his right palm.

"Yep," Donnie admitted to our teacher, "but you should'a seen the other guy." The boy twinkled. Mrs. S. twinkled back at his joke. I could see right away why Mrs. Shaw was everyone's favorite teacher.

Thelma and I hung back at the end of the line, and we inched forward as Mrs. Shaw took time to greet each of the eighteen kids ahead of us, one at a time. She knew everyone . . . everyone but us. I felt like I had "Does Not Belong" smeared all over my face. But Mrs. Shaw was having none of that.

"And of course you are Thelma and Carol!" Our teacher threw out her arms to take us both in when it was our turn. "Come on, let's get this year started." She ushered us into Room Eleven.

"Wow!" We breathed out our surprise and wonder. Mrs. Shaw was an artist, and her room—our room—showed her talent. A gigantic picture announcing "Fall Is Here!" covered half the window wall directly across from the door. Mrs. Shaw had used colored chalk to make the browns and reds and yellows of fall, which might sound boring and ordinary, but Mrs. S. could line and smudge and work chalk into a masterpiece. Really.

She had made magic in the Geography Center too, but with colored pencils and crayons instead of chalk. Her hand-drawn maps reached from ceiling to floor. Without asking, we knew which countries we would study. And the pictures she drew on the maps made them come alive with stories. A girl from Mexico patted round tortillas between her palms. A boy in Africa fished the river with a net. I had never known such wonderful things could come from a crayon box.

Mrs. Shaw's creations invited us around the room—her book-jacket collage said, "Read me," and her crazy cutout numbers made even arithmetic look fun—but the Art Center was the best of everything. A double-sided easel stood ready. Shelves of paints waited, and clean brushes stood tall in jars. Stacks of multicolored construction paper just needed scissors, and a roll of white newsprint stood ready to unwind a mural all around the room if we wanted. Mrs. Shaw expected us to be creative.

And we soon found out that October was our big chance to bust out our creative side. The Village of Hilliard wanted the town done up for the annual Halloween Street Carnival. The village council contacted Mr. Moore, Mr. Moore talked to Mrs. Shaw, and the plan was set. All the store owners on Main Street agreed to have their front windows painted with Halloween scenes, and we kids would be the painters, or at least some of us would be.

"Anyone can submit a design." Mrs. Shaw encouraged us like we were real artists. "The village council will select ten of the best for the store windows." She primed our imaginations before we took to paper. "What do you think Halloween looks like? What are the colors? What is the mood? Scary? Happy? How can you show it? All right, artists, let's get to work!"

Our tempera-paint witches and pumpkins would decorate the storefronts along Main Street from Ginny's Beauty Shop to Huffman's IGA, from Willbarger's Drug Store (which, I later discovered, had an ice-cream soda fountain!) to Arch Alder's Garage and Adkins' Barber Shop on the corners of the alley. Even the plate glass of Turney's Pool Hall would sport a witch or two. We set to work on our designs.

"Now that's an interesting scene," Mrs. Shaw encouraged as she passed by our desks. "You might add an orange pumpkin or two in the corn shocks and some red in the leaves. The color would add interest."

All twenty of us hunched over our drawings, intent on toothy jack-o'-lanterns and ghosts popping from windows. My picture showed two up-to-no-good witches beside a steamy cauldron. Their broomsticks stood waiting just out of the fire's light. A yellow disk moon rose behind dark, bare-branch trees that I draped with red-eyed cats (black, of course) and upside-down bats hanging from low branches. A dry field dotted with cornstalks and orange pumpkins filled the distant background. Misty clouds drifted through the night sky and into the shadowy trees to give everything an eerie feel. Altogether it was a spooky situation, and I was satisfied with the results.

"You have until tomorrow to submit your final draw-ing for the contest," Mrs. S. reminded us, "so take time to do your finest work." I turned in my "finest" with all the others and waited three days for the village council judges to con-sider all the entries. Finally Mr. Moore stood at the morning assembly to announce the names of the artists who would represent Hilliard School.

"Margie Anderson, Dennis Woodruff, Nancy Good," he called out, "Carla Feldpausch, Connie Conklin . . ." I dropped my head lower. "Carol Richardson . . ." I didn't hear the last names. My witches and bats would fly across one of the store windows in town for the Halloween Street Carni-val—that was all I needed to know!

On Friday, October 24, a week before the carnival, we ten newly appointed street artists carried Halloween colors— forty-six quart jars in all—to Mr. Moore's new blue Chevy, along with brushes, extra jars for mixing colors, plenty of cleanup rags, and a hefty stack of old Dispatch newspapers to catch sidewalk spills.

"You could do all of downtown Columbus with this much paint," Mr. Moore joked while hefting boxes of tem-pera-filled jars into the trunk. He carefully closed the lid when all the supplies were secured. "I'll meet you in front of Adkins' Barber Shop." He dropped into the driver's seat and rolled down the window. The ten of us started the walk along

Main Street to the "uptown" section of Hilliard, which was what we called the collection of stores and businesses that was the main part of town.

We passed Billy Tallman's house across from the school. Billy was in my class, but I didn't know much about him. He went home every day for lunch and didn't come back for after-lunch recess. He never raised his hand to answer questions in class, and he couldn't spell the words when it was his turn at the Monday spelling bee. Mrs. S. went around the class to practice the week's spelling list, and Billy mumbled out the wrong letters every time. No one expected him to get it right anymore.

"His mother ran away with a Fuller Brush man." Macie repeated what her neighbor had said. "Broke Mr. Tallman's heart, and he left to go find her. Neither of 'em ever came back, not his mother or his daddy. Guess that makes Billy an orphan or somethin'," Macie finished with an in-the-know flourish. Seemed like an awful thing, unthinkable even— moms and dads didn't just leave without taking their kids. I wasn't sure if what Macie said was true, but it bothered me to think it could be. What I did know was that Billy lived with a grandmother we never saw, and he always kept to himself.

After Billy's house, Main Street took a sharp curve to the right and headed past Carey's Store where they sold Luden's cherry cough drops at the front counter and fried egg sandwiches in the back. The post office was across the street along with Russell's grain elevator. We walked past them all and then over the railroad tracks to the main business part of Hilliard. Adkins' Barber Shop stood next to Winteringer's Dry Goods, which sold everything from bib overalls for farmers to two-for-a-penny candy for kids. The M&M Restaurant was right across the street beside The Red and White Grocery, with its overhead fans that stirred the stale-fish air around and made the whole store smell nasty.

Mr. Moore's Chevy was already parked in front of Adkins' when we got there, and Mrs. Shaw, who had ridden in the Chevy's front seat, had already divided the paints, brushes, rags, and newspapers we would need to take to our painting locations.

"Margie, you do the IGA. Dennis, do Willbarger's Drug Store, and Carol, take your supplies and get started on Ginny's." Mrs. S. was all business as she barked out the assigned windows and sent us on our way. She expected serious dedication and good results from this "hooky day" away from regular school.

I spread out newspapers on the sidewalk in front of Ginny's Beauty Shop. The shop was by itself at the far end of Main Street. "Hey, Nancy," I yelled and waved at my nearest artist neighbor. She stood in front of McMillian's Hardware on the corner of Main and Norwich, a long block from Ginny's.

"Hey back." Nancy fluttered a wave and a quick smile, but she didn't stop looking at the glass "canvas" in front of her. Nancy was nice, and we were a little bit friends, but I wished it was Thelma in front of the hardware store. We would have run back and forth between the two stores to admire my witches and her jack-o'-lanterns. But Thelma's drawing wasn't chosen.

So without Thelma, I set to work instead of chatting. While I arranged my paint jars in strategic spots where they would be easy to reach, I flitted glances through the window at the goings-on inside the shop. One woman, maybe Ginny herself, stood over a gray-haired customer in a swivel chair. Half the woman's hair was wrapped in tight pink curlers, and the maybe-Ginny woman worked her fingers deftly to finish wrapping the other half. Two women sat in fat stuffed chairs against the wall and leafed through magazines. White helmets hung low over their heads and covered everything to the bottom of their ears. I wasn't sure what was happening under the helmets but determined to figure it out before the day was over.

I had never been inside Ginny's Beauty Shop or any beauty shop for that matter. Mom cut my hair with a special pair of scissors that she got free with her Raleigh cigarette coupons. Every pack of Raleighs had a coupon slipped behind the cellophane wrapper, and a twelve-pack carton of Raleighs had a bonus coupon strip. Mom saved up, and when she had enough coupons, she ordered something from the Raleigh redemption catalog. The hair scissors had cost 350 coupons.

I had gotten a haircut the day the scissors came in the mailbox. But even with the special shears, Mom couldn't cut bangs. They were gapped and raggedy, and when she tried to "even them up," they just got shorter and shorter until they spiked straight out at the top of my forehead. "I chop hair; I don't cut it," Mom admitted. But a Ginny's haircut cost money we didn't have.

I wasn't thinking much about Ginny haircuts as I stood in front of the shop on Friday, October 24. Instead, I was thinking about how big the Ginny window was. It would take all day, and jars and jars of paint, to cover that much space.

And that's exactly how it went. It was three o'clock before we all were done. The hot Indian summer sun of late October beat down on us as we took a Main Street art tour to see what we had accomplished. Our paintings were spectacular! We all agreed on that, even—and especially—Mrs. S. and Mr. Moore. "We are so proud," they both beamed. "You've certainly done your part to get our town ready for Halloween." We walked back to school happy and got there just in time to catch the bus home.

"How was school?" Mom was at our kitchen sink peeling potatoes to fry for supper.

"Good." I had already changed into dungarees and hung my school dress in the wardrobe. "Mrs. Shaw likes art and she's really good at it." I tied my apron in back so I could help with supper. I didn't mention the Ginny window because I wanted it to be a surprise if we got to go to the Halloween Street Carnival. Daddy would probably have to work late, but I was hoping not.

"Get those sliced." Mom pointed with her chin to some fat yellow onions on the table. "Then you can go play if you want." She set the rules. "Unless you have homework, but I guess it can wait since it's Friday." She relented even before I protested.

After onions, I hung upside down while I waited to be called in for supper. The pear tree between the fence and the old well in the backyard was my favorite hang place. The tree didn't have any fruit on it—Daddy had said it needed another pear tree nearby to produce—but it did have a low, straight limb that was as thick as a man's arm and strong enough to hold my weight. I shinnied up the trunk, looped my right leg and then the left over the limb, and did a backward somersault so I could hang by my crooked knees.

"You draining your brain, Sweet Potato?" Daddy's flannel-shirt belly came into view. I could hear the tease in his voice. Upside-down Daddy stepped backward and squatted down so he was at my eye level. He lowered himself onto the concrete slab that covered the old, dry well.

"Nah, just looking at things different." I reversed the somersault so my butt was sitting on the branch. From that position, I jumped and hit the ground at the base of the tree. Daddy patted his knee, and I took a seat there so we could talk.

"How was school?" Daddy's left arm hugged my shoulder.

"Can we go to the Halloween Street Carnival next Friday?" I dodged past the question and snuggled closer to smell the Old Spice aftershave on his cheeks. Daddy always took a shower and changed clothes at the shop before he came home. Old Spice was his clean smell, like cloves and something else I couldn't name.

"Don't know, little girl. We'll have to see," he dodged back. "We'll go if I don't have overtime. That's the best I can say." He threw in a little hope when he read my disappointment. I knew overtime beat everything else because it paid time and a half, so I didn't ask anymore.

Friday night rain turned into a frosty gleam on Saturday morning. It made the trees and bushes sparkle, and it wilted the last of the zinnias that grew along the south side of the house and had been spared from earlier frosts. The sun warmed the air after lunch, and I scoured the field for one last bouquet of prairie flowers and seed tassels. Fall was slow-stepping toward winter.

On Sunday morning I startled awake to Mom's yelling. "Ross! Ross!" I heard an excited scramble in the kitchen. We all had slept a little later than usual. It was a lazy day because Daddy didn't have to go to work—no double-time shift at the shop for a change—but something caused Mom to yell into our dozing.

"Ross!" she called again as Jerry and I thumped our way down from upstairs. By the time we got to the kitchen, Daddy and Mom stood armed. Daddy hoisted a broom and Mom held a wet dish rag spread between her hands. Both looked down at the floor. "There's a mouse loose in here." Mom didn't take her eyes from searching. "It jumped out of the bread drawer when I opened it. Scared the daylights outta me."

The day before, Mom had found the corner chewed off the loaf of bread when she went to make breakfast toast, so we knew we had a mouse. It was fall and not a surprise that the outside critters were trying to get inside where it was warm, but Mom said, "We're not going to be a hotel for mice even if we do live in the country." She was strong on the subject of mice. So before bed on Saturday, Daddy baited a trap with peanut butter and set it inside the bread drawer for the night.

"As soon as I walked into the kitchen, I heard the trap snap," Mom said, still searching the floor for movement, "so I opened the drawer. Out jumped the mouse. Scared the daylights outta me," she repeated. "Help us find it," she directed.

So Jerry and I joined the search, trailing our eyes slowly from corner to corner along the bottom gap where the pasteboard wall hit the scoured planks of the kitchen floor. Just as we were about to give up, Jerry spotted a little fuzzy gray movement. "There!" he pointed. "There, under the table."

"I got 'im." Daddy got the broom in position to flatten the mouse. "Eva, wave the rag at his behind to get 'im movin.'"

The mouse took off before Mom could flap the rag. Daddy banged the broom down hard but missed, and the mouse careened across the floor, running for its life. It made it to the throw rug by the sink.

Aha, thought the mouse, *a hiding place!* and quickly tucked half, the head half, of his body under the edge of the rug. In mouse-think, the danger was gone because he couldn't see it anymore. His eyes were covered and blind to the situation, but we could see his tail twitching innocently at the end of his butt, which was still sticking out from under the rug.

"Mmmm." Daddy held the broom uncertainly.

"Mmmm." Mom watched the innocently twitching tail. We were all frozen—Daddy with the broom, Mom with the killing rag meant to ensnare the bread thief, Jerry and I with nothing but our thoughts, and the mouse, who was convinced he was safe.

"We can't kill 'im." I pleaded his case. "It wouldn't be fair. He doesn't know."

"But we can't just let 'im go." Mom spoke without conviction.

"Mmmm," Daddy hummed again, just as the mouse, perhaps finally correctly assessing his situation and sensing our wavering, took off running again. This time he raced out of the kitchen, through the bedroom where Daddy and Mom slept, and under the flimsy door that led up the stairs. Daddy didn't broom him, Mom didn't rag him, and Jerry and I stepped aside to let him pass. After the mousecapade, we stored the bread in a metal bread box and didn't set any more traps that winter.

The rest of Sunday passed uneventfully, and then it was Monday and time for the school bus. I was eager and went to the end of the drive early. I wanted to see the Ginny window again, and I wanted to show it off to Thelma.

The bus rumbled on forever, scooping up its riders one by one. By October the seating arrangements had been silently settled among us, and no one took the spot beside me, knowing it was for Thelma, who boarded at the end of the trip. Thelma was all smiles and gangly legs when she finally swung on and plopped down next to me. "Brought ya somethin'." She handed me a small lidded box.

"What is it?" I was surprised.

"Open hit up an' see," Thelma teased. By the way she handled the box, I knew something delicate was inside, delicate and special. I lifted the cover carefully.

Right away I knew the moth was a Cecropia. It lay like a swatch of fine silk cloth, its reddish body and powdery, black-brown wings outlined in white and red. Its full-spread wings covered the cotton on the bottom of the box. It was huge, at least six inches across. "Oh! Thelma! Where did you find it?"

"Front porch. Light must'a brung hit in last night. 'Twas flung out dead on ta' screen this mornin', like hit was waitin'. I knowed ya'd like hit."

"Like it" hardly described what I felt. The moth was a remarkable treasure, and as it turned out, a miraculous gift timed perfectly because it took some of the sting out of what came next.

As our school bus rolled on toward Main Street, I was excited, and Thelma could tell. "Ginny's window? That ta' one ya did?" I nodded and peered ahead intently as we took the curve that turned Avery Road into Main Street. Just a few blocks to go, then the beauty shop came into sight. The bus lumbered on. Thelma and I planted noses against the glass, waiting to catch our first glimpse of the witches plotting mayhem over the cauldron in Ginny's window.

But there was no cauldron. No fire. No witches stirring their brew. No bare trees so carefully brushed. My painting had vanished. Ginny's window was clean, clear, and shiny. "It's gone," I whispered to myself, stunned.

"'Tis gone," Thelma whispered back. "Whatever happened ta' hit?"

"Don't know." I watched miserably as we passed McMillian's Hardware, Huffman's IGA, Willbarger's Drug Store, Alder's Garage, Adkins' Barber Shop, Winterringer's Dry Goods, and Turney's Pool Hall on the way toward school. All had jack-o'-lanterns and bats intact. Ginny's window, my window, was the only one washed clean.

"I'm real sorry, Carol" was all Thelma offered. What else was there to say?

At school I tried to lose myself in Mrs. Shaw's science experiment. It was something about air pressure in a vacuum and balloons bursting because of it, but I couldn't focus. What had happened to my painting? I wanted to know.

Or maybe I didn't. What if the village council had decided my tempera was too drippy and sent some volunteer fireman to wash it away? Or what if my witches had cast a spell of botched haircuts or frizzy perms? Surely Ginny had had to undo the curse by the light of the moon with her bucket and mop? Or worse, what if Mrs. S. and Mr. Moore had changed their minds and decided my work reflected poorly on the school? Maybe they gave Ginny's the wash-down rather than be embarrassed.

I deserved to know why my painting was the only one singled out for the hose treatment. I wanted answers, but in the end I couldn't risk them. Mrs. Shaw offered nothing. Mr. Moore said nothing. I asked nothing. Perhaps they thought I didn't know. I pretended I didn't.

Later I wrote the whole miserable event down in my story tablet to try to figure it out. It felt like I had done something wrong, like it was my fault somehow, but I couldn't see how. I had done my best. Turned out that Daddy had to work overtime on Friday night, and for once I was glad. No one mentioned that we missed the Halloween Street Carnival. Two months later, Christmas decorations helped me figure out what happened to my painting and why.

A New World Thanksgiving

The Indian summer of Halloween turned bitter two days into November. We went from short sleeves to winter bundles without the usual easing-into-it weather transition. The truck came from Russell's Feed and Grain just in time to beat the cold and dumped three tons of dusty, black coal just the other side of the fence in the backyard. I wondered if some of Thelma's people had dug it out of a Kentucky mine. Daddy stoked both stoves every morning before he left for the shop, and by the time Jerry and I got up, their cast-iron bellies glowed on the outside and popped and sizzled within.

For breakfast Mom laid slices of white bread on the top of the front-room stove and left them there until they turned toasty brown and crumbly crisp. We spread the slices with butter and slathered them with blackberry jam from our surprise summer patch.

During the first week of November, turkeys and Pilgrims showed up on Mrs. Shaw's bulletin board at school, and Miss Roberts, our music teacher, pounded out the notes to "Over the River and through the Woods" while we sang with gusto, trying to stay warm in her cold little classroom off the gym.

November blew on deeper into the month, and we hunkered down to the reality of the gray Ohio winter that stretched out before us. The cold blistered the playground, frosted the swings, and slicked the slide. At recess we huddled in small groups near the building, waiting for the bell to ring us inside.

In the warm classroom, Mrs. Shaw was full of peppy talk about the First Thanksgiving. "Squanto taught the Pilgrims how to survive the first winter in the New World," she told us. "He showed them the Indian way to fertilize corn plants with fish and hunt wild turkeys for meat." Mrs. S. held up a picture of a tall, lean man with few clothes, and feathers in his braided hair. "The Pilgrims would have died if the Indians hadn't helped them." She made the point stronger. "So they decided to have a feast to celebrate the good harvest and to thank Squanto and the other Indians. That was the very first Thanksgiving," our teacher said, tying the story with a bow.

Then she added, "Now the fun part." We waited. "The whole school will reenact the First Thanksgiving the day before break!" The news did cheer us from our winter slump.

"We'll have no regular classes the Wednesday before Thanks-giving!" Even more cheer for us.

Mrs. Shaw went on to explain how the women who cooked our lunch had agreed to fix cranberries and other First Thanksgiving food. "We will do the research about what the menu might have been in 1621." Mrs. S. broke out the study part of the project for us. "But it's not just food we want to learn about; we also want to know what people wore then. Soooo . . ." Mrs. Shaw drew out the word for dramatic effect. "We can make our own costumes," she finished with a flourish. Some of us would dress up as Pilgrims and others as Indians. One person would be Squanto.

I knew right away that I wanted to play Squanto. He definitely was the best person in the First Thanksgiving story. I decided that, even though I knew from a book I had read that Squanto's help turned out to be a bad thing for the Indians in the end. A lot of white people like the Pilgrims came to the New World after that First Thanksgiving. Of course, the world wasn't really "new," because the Indians had lived there for thousands of years. But the white people pushed the Indians out of their homes anyway and stole all their land. Many brought killer diseases with them, and the Indians got sick and died from the germs the white people brought. Squanto's whole tribe died of smallpox.

So all in all, it was a miserable deal for the Indians when the Pilgrims arrived. But Squanto didn't know all that when he taught the Mayflower folks how to plant and fish. He was just doing what seemed neighborly and right. That's why I wanted to be Squanto in the First Thanksgiving reenactment. But being a girl—and the Ginny's window girl at that—I figured I wouldn't get the part. I decided on the next best thing: an Indian woman.

Deciding was one thing. Doing was another. I scoured the history books that Mrs. Shaw brought in for us to use, but I could not find any pictures of Indian women at the 1621 feast. The paintings showed lots of Pilgrims, both men and women (though mostly men) and some Indian braves like Squanto, but no women. Surely the Indian women had come to the thanks-for-helping-us dinner. They'd probably even fixed a lot of the food and cleaned up after, but where were they? Did the artists forget to draw them into the paintings? Mrs. Shaw was as stumped as I was. It was like the Indian women were invisible or didn't exist.

It seemed that if I wanted to represent an Indian woman at the First Thanksgiving, I was on my own for the costume. I went to Mom for help. "What about this, Carol?" Mom flared out a skirt she had found in her packed-away clothes box. "This might do." She considered the skirt's soft brown cloth that could, I decided, pass for buckskin hide. Buckskin was the best idea I had come up with. The Indian men wore buckskin, so maybe the women did too.

The top part of my costume was another problem. The

pictures of the men didn't help because the men were mostly naked on the top—just bead necklaces and a few feathers. Again, the packed-away clothes box held the answer. Mom pulled out a white slip-over blousy top with long, puffy sleeves. The fabric was thin and coarse like someone had made it by hand. It had a fringy collar that covered the blouse front and back and hung low on the arms. The fringe was almost like a shawl. I tried it with the "buckskin" skirt and it was perfect, or at least as close as I could get.

"What about braids?" Mrs. Shaw asked when I told her about my costume. "You need braids." She had pointed out the obvious, but my hair was short, curly, and blonde, not long, black, and glossy as I imagined the Indian women had. "Let me think on it." Mrs. S. frowned. "Horsehair would look authentic, but we couldn't get enough. Yarn, maybe." That decided things.

Mrs. Shaw pulled out her art smarts, and overnight she made a very respectable yarn wig with long, black braids. "Try it on," she directed the next morning when I arrived at school. "Not bad." She appraised my wigged head. "Needs beads and some feathers."

Everyone loved the wig, so Mrs. S. made five more before reenactment Wednesday, one for everyone who signed up to play an Indian part, not counting Thelma who had her own dark braids. One of the five extra wigs was for Squanto. As things happened, the wigs were so special the Pilgrims wanted to switch to being Indians, but Mrs. Shaw said no. So for reenactment Wednesday at least, the Indians got the better deal.

As promised, we had no regular school on the Wednesday before Thanksgiving break because the entire day was dedicated to the reenactment. We came dressed in our costumes and went directly from the bus to the lunchroom for assembly. Mr. Moore had on a tall Pilgrim hat and black coat and even Pilgrim buckles on his shoes. He had gone all out. The teachers, including the Triple M, were dressed as Pilgrims too, but Mrs. Shaw was different. She joined Thelma and me as the only other Indian woman.

"Mrs. S. is one a' us," Thelma whispered.

"Yep." I smiled. We were surprised and proud. Mrs. Shaw threw us a wink on the side.

Each grade had stage time at the assembly. First Grade gobbled through a Thanksgiving turkey song while Miss Roberts beamed. Second Grade recited a poem, also about turkeys. Third Grade skipped the turkeys and did a funny skit about a pumpkin that turned into a pie.

The assembly went on and on until it was our time to take the stage. We had the serious job of telling the story of the First Thanksgiving. The tale wound on from the Mayflower landing to the 1621 feast. Squanto played a big part, of course, but it was President Abraham Lincoln who brought things to a close even though he came later in history and wasn't even there for the real First Thanksgiving. Tall and skinny Honest Abe stepped out on stage at the very end with a proclamation that made Thanksgiving official. "And that's why we celebrate Thanksgiving even to this day," Mr. Moore summed up after Abe had finished his proclaiming. "Now it's time to eat." We let out a big whoop!

We gobbled and stuffed ourselves until the orange bus pulled up to carry us home. "Your costume do okay?" Mom wanted to know when I came through the door.

"Mrs. Shaw was an Indian woman too," I answered with a flush of pride. "She let me keep the wig." I modeled the braids for Mom.

"Looks good." She rubbed the black yarn between her fingers. "Now get your clothes changed and help me in the kitchen." The wig conversation was over.

◆◆◆

There was lots to do to get ready for our Thanksgiving even though we wouldn't eat until evening because Daddy had to go into the shop on Thursday, same as always. Columbus Auto Parts was closed on Thanksgiving, but Daddy was a millwright. His job was to keep all the machines working so there was no slowdown on the production line. He saved big repair jobs for times when the shop was closed and the machines were not needed.

"Got a piston machine that's giving the men some trouble," Daddy reported. "I need to tear it down and find out what's wrong. We got a big contract with Chevy coming up." Daddy took his work seriously. And Thanksgiving work paid double time, so we planned our family dinner for six when he got home.

Some kids at school bragged about how big their Thanksgiving turkey would be. Thelma and I listened, but didn't talk, and for sure did not brag. Neither of our families raised turkeys, and we certainly couldn't afford a store-bought bird. The main dish for the Richardson family dinner was lying on the frozen dirt floor in the garage, waiting to be picked, skinned, gutted, and cleaned.

Daddy had killed our dinner. He had suited up early Wednesday morning, nestled the twelve-gauge shotgun in the crook of his arm, put his dogs on the leash, and headed to the back field to hunt. It meant getting in late to work, but he had arranged to take a later shift. Over oatmeal before school, Jerry and I could hear Bess and Blue's deep-throated brays coming from the back of our acres. "They picked up somethin'." Jerry cocked his head to the sound.

"Best trackin' beagles I ever had." Daddy always bragged to friends about Bess and Blue. "Best rabbit dogs in the county." He upped the ante. Daddy always had dogs tied up out back, and always beagles. He had gotten Bess and Blue for forty dollars from an old man off Rings Road on the other side of Hilliard. Forty dollars was a lot of money, but "it was a good deal," Daddy said. "The man was givin' up his dogs— got too old to run 'em anymore—and wanted me to have 'em." So Bess and Blue had come to live on Leap Road with us, and the day before Thanksgiving they went with Daddy to hunt for our dinner. They did their jobs well, and two rabbits and a pheasant lay cold in the garage, waiting for Daddy to dress them when he got home from the shop on Wednesday night.

Pumpkin pie spice tickled my nose when I woke up Thursday morning. Mom was already baking. "Got to get the pies done early," she explained when I hit the kitchen. "That pheasant's going to take some time to fix."

I saw the naked bird in a roasting pan next to the sink. Its glorious, shimmering feathers were long gone, and I could see the sharp red marks on its skin, left from the shotgun pellets. I also noticed the cut-up rabbit in a bowl of salt water in the sink. The same red blotches marked the rabbit skin. Mom dug the metal pellets out of the meat as best she could before she cooked it, but I knew to be on the lookout when eating time came.

After a quick trip to the outhouse, I washed my hands and got started peeling potatoes. We would boil them soft and mash them later with hot milk and butter. Mom worked on the pheasant.

"Get the matches, Carol." She held the naked bird in her hands and pointed with her chin. "I'll hold the bird while you burn off the pin feathers." I struck the long kitchen match on the side of the box and ran the flame over the pheasant's pale, naked skin. Tiny bursts of sparks jumped from wisps of feathers that still clung to the bird. "Phew." Mom wrinkled her nose to close out the nasty smell of burnt feathers. I held my breath and waited for the stink to drift away.

Mom stuffed a whole apple and a peeled onion into the clean bird and brushed melted butter all over the upturned breast and the lean legs that stuck out on the sides. The beautiful cock pheasant that once soared free over our eight acres was ready for the oven. I knew I should be glad.

"What do you think about cloverleaf rolls?" Mom asked, already knowing the answer. She measured flour and salt, then mixed in the bubbly yeast and warm water. She covered the pale-yellow dough with a damp cloth. "Set this to rise in a warm spot behind the stove in the front room." Mom passed me the bowl. "Then you finish them, Carol." When the soft, eggy dough was doubled, I punched it down, pulled off walnut-size pieces and placed them, three to a cup, in a muffin pan. When all twelve cups were full, I brushed melted butter carefully on the tops and returned the pan to its warm spot behind the stove. Soon the smell of working yeast filled the house. "Make sure those go in the oven right before dinner." Mom eyed the pan of rolls. "We want 'em hot and crispy on the table." My mouth watered.

The Dodge coasted into the drive close to six. "I can taste pheasant already," Daddy boomed as soon as he opened the kitchen door. He was rosy cheeked and swimmy eyed, and in a smiley mood.

"You been nippin', Ross?" Mom gave him a question and an accusing look.

"Just a one beer, Eva." He moved in to hug her. "Couple a' guys from the shop wanted to buy me one."

"More than one" was all she said as she sidestepped the hug. "Get your coat off. Dinner's ready." She let it go. I was glad. Everything could get tense when they talked about beer. Sometimes Mom would dish out the silent treatment and barely talk to Daddy for days. Jerry and I knew to stay clear, or we could be swept into the silence as well.

But the moment passed and Thanksgiving was not ruined. I let out my breath in relief as the dinner conversation smoothed out to normal. "Pheasant's moist and tender, Eva." Daddy smacked down his second helping. "And the rabbit tastes mild." He pulled some dark thigh meat off with his fingers. "Wild meat can taste gamey if it's not cooked right." Mom knew he was right and was pleased with the praise.

"Any more rolls?" Jerry searched the table. I took the bread basket to the oven and refilled it with the last six cloverleafs. The outsides were glossy brown from the butter brushing, and the insides were tender soft.

"Just one more." Mom passed the full basket to Jerry and then to me. I pulled the three "leafs" apart and spread butter and blackberry jam on each one.

The basket stopped at Daddy, and he put the last two rolls onto his plate. "Pass that good gravy, Eva," Daddy clucked in anticipation. He liked to top his meal with bread sopped in silky meat-juice gravy. Seemed like a waste of good cloverleafs to me, but for Daddy it was like being back on the farm in North Carolina.

Our bellies ached, but we stretched them a bit more to end with two choices for dessert: pumpkin pie or, my favorite, apple turnovers. After all the bowls and plates stood empty and the pheasant was nothing but bones, Daddy pushed away from the table and headed for his chair in the front room. Jerry followed and sprawled on the davenport for a nap. Mom and I stayed in the kitchen and began the long, messy cleanup. I thought about the "invisible" Indian women at the First Thanksgiving.

Mom and I hurried along with the washing and drying so we could finish by nine o'clock in time for our radio program. We just made it as Daddy tuned in the Philco to NBC. "The National Broadcasting Company presents *The Adventures of Sam Spade, Detective.*" The deep voice of the radio announcer vibrated into our Ohio house and drew us in. We settled down to a half-hour show put on by radio actors who took us on the mesmerizing journey of "The Terrified Turkey Caper."

"Good program," Daddy yawned and reached to turn the radio knob to "off" when the story was done and the Pepsodent toothpaste jingle took over.

"Sam Spade's my favorite detective on radio," I yawned back as we all shuffled for our shoes. "He always solves the crime."

"Yep, he does," Daddy agreed as he lifted the lid on the front-room stove to shovel in more coal for the night. Jerry and I headed upstairs for bed as Daddy finished filling the bedroom stove. Mom turned back the covers and crawled in. She'd had a long day.

I woke Friday to the sound of an animal screaming. Or I thought it was an animal. But finally I realized it was the wind blasting the back of the house and raging around the corners and sides—the sound was nothing I'd ever heard before. The bedroom window was still dark like the middle of the night, but I was sure it must be morning. My toes were frozen in their socks, and my breath was like smoke in the cold air. The coal-stove heat did not go to the second floor. I didn't want to get up, but I threw back the covers in a burst and ran for the steps to get where it was warm.

"Bad storm," Mom said as she shoveled coal into the stoves. I wished I'd brought my blanket from the bed; even downstairs was cold.

"Where's Daddy?" I wondered why Mom was building the morning fires.

"Putting snow chains on the Dodge so he can go to work." Mom pulled her sweater tighter and walked toward the kitchen. I smelled perking coffee on the stove.

Getting snow chains on the car was a tricky job, especially for one person. I watched out the front window as Daddy fought the wind to lay one of the contraptions flat on the ground. It looked like a ladder with two long side chains and cross-chain rungs every foot or so. When he had it perfectly straight, he lifted it and draped it over the Dodge's rear tire.

Then came the hardest part: he started the engine and eased the car back. He was careful to keep the draped chain on the moving tire but expose the loose ends so he could hook them in place around the tire when he got out. It was slow, tedious work to get four wheels chained up. Daddy looked whipped when he came through the kitchen door.

"Snow's already deep and it's just getting started." He stamped his feet on the throw rug. "I better get outta here before it gets any worse. Stewart'll wonder where I am." Stewart was Mr. Stewart. He worked at the shop, too, and lived on Jeanette Road about halfway down from Leap. Mr. Stewart and Daddy alternated weeks for driving. Too bad it was Daddy's week. He grabbed his lunch box and headed into the storm.

A weak light filtered in from outside as we huddled around the front-room stove. Mom said we'd eat breakfast there to stay closer to the fire. No matter how much coal she put in, the stoves couldn't dent the cold. Icy pellets scoured the windows, and wind coming in through the cracks blew the curtains. The panes were iced over on the inside and made spidery webs of crystal that etched the glass. Radio reception was so scratchy we finally turned it off and settled under our blankets on the davenport to read.

I had just put down Nancy Drew and found scissors to cut paper snowflakes when the kitchen door banged open. "What on earth?" Mom started, thinking the door had blown open. Then we heard a door bang shut and a loud, raspy voice.

"Eva! Eva!" It was Daddy.

"What on earth?" Mom repeated, and we all rushed to the kitchen. Daddy was a snowman but not a jolly one. Every part of him was frozen icy white.

"Let me get to the stove." He was shedding his frozen coat on the way to the glowing heat. We all helped him get his gloves off, and his work boots—it took some time to un-lace the icy strings. Finally he stood as close to the fire as he could without touching it. First he warmed his front, then backside, then front again.

"What happened?" Mom asked our question.

"Tell you in a minute," he rasped, "but I gotta warm up some first." Mom handed him some hot coffee heated up from breakfast.

"I've never seen a storm this bad." He shook his head like he couldn't believe it even though he had been in it. "I started out on Leap to get Stewart," he began. "Snow was blowin' so bad I couldn't see the road. Thought about com-ing back home, but nowhere to turn around." He spit out the story in cold bursts. "Nothing to do but keep going and hope

I could make it. I ran into the ditch somewhere up the road. Couldn't get the car out no matter what I did. Chains didn't help in the drifts. Don't know if I even made it to Jeanette. No way to tell. Couldn't see anything—not the houses or the mailboxes, the road, nothing."

"How'd you make it back?" Again, our question from Mom.

"I got lucky is all I can figure." His smile had warmed up a little. "When I couldn't get the car back on the road, I started walking. Never woulda found the house if it hadn't been for the big elms in the yard. Even the storm couldn't hide them. Saw 'em sticking up like markers and I followed 'em home." That was all he told us then, though we knew there must be a lot more to the story. He could have lost his way and frozen to death trying to walk back, but none of us said it.

The storm rattled and screamed all day Friday and into the night. On Saturday, it got even worse. The temperature dropped so low inside we turned on the spigot and let the water trickle so it wouldn't freeze solid in the pipe. Around noon on Saturday, Daddy had to go out to the pile for more coal. We kept a good supply in the house but had used it all to keep the stoves going. "I had to dig out the coal pile before I could fill the buckets," Daddy reported when he came in. "The drifts next to the fence are up to my waist." He made several trips back until there was a sizable pile of coal on the garage floor. "Better bring it in now while I still can," he said.

"Way this storm's blowin', the whole house might get covered before it's done."

When he finally came in to get warm, I could see worry on him. "Hope Bess and Blue are okay." There it was. He shook snow off his coat. "Nothin' to do about it 'cause I can't get to 'em."

"Let's stir up a batch of cookies." Mom broke into the dog worry and surprised us with a lighthearted idea. We all knew she wanted to get Daddy's mind off his beagles and our thoughts away from the howling wind. "The oven will warm up the kitchen a little too," she reasoned, always practical.

Mom turned on the gas to light the oven, and I got mixing bowls from the shelf along with the flour and brown sugar. Before long the house smelled warm and peanut buttery. We laid out the hot, fresh-from-the-oven treats on a towel, but they were in our stomachs before they cooled. The wind howled outside, but creamy peanut butter cookies took some of the worry away. Mom's idea worked.

The storm raged on into the night, and the story made the radio news on Sunday morning. The National Broadcasting Company reported that Ohio was being hit with a record blizzard. "By late in the day Saturday, snow reached nearly two feet in parts of Ohio, with some areas recording drifts as deep as twenty-five feet," the announcer intoned. We sat hunched over the Philco, listening for any scrap of information about the storm that howled on outside.

The winds slacked off some by Monday afternoon, but the news was worse. We wrapped ourselves in blankets and huddled around the radio in the front room. The stove crackled but did little to cut the cold. The NBC announcer came on air: "The winter storm pounding the state of Ohio has piled up snow depths totaling nearly three feet. Bulldozers are being used to clear roads for ambulances. The governor has called out the Ohio National Guard to use jeeps to transport people to the hospital and deliver food to hard-hit rural areas."

"We should check on Mrs. Murdock, Ross." Mom was concerned.

Daddy agreed. "I'll go over as soon as this is over."

"Wires and trees were blown down by winds that reached sixty miles an hour," the NBC radio announcer continued. "Many buildings collapsed under the weight of the snow." Mom switched off the Philco as the broadcast turned to other news. We felt lucky that our roof, our trees, and our power lines remained intact.

Daddy kept both stoves glowing, and on Monday night we all slept downstairs where it was warmer. "The upstairs is just too cold," Mom said. We found out she was right when we hurried to bring down more covers before bed. The upstairs windowpanes were solid ice.

The sun broke through on Tuesday, and we woke to the sound of the county snowplow on Leap Road. Jerry and I cheered. "Thank God." Mom was relieved. Daddy was chomping to check on Bess and Blue and to find the Dodge. He wanted get it out of the ditch, so he was glad to hear the plow.

"I've missed too much work already." He poured milk into his coffee until it overflowed into the saucer. "Not sure how ole man Klages is goin' to handle this." Daddy scooped fried eggs up with his fork. "He might try and dock us all for not showing up." Ole man Klages was Reynold Klages, the owner of the Columbus Auto Parts Company.

"You mean not pay you? For not getting to work through the snowstorm?" Mom was angry at the very idea. "You could've died trying to get there! Nobody could've made it in. Not even Klages!" She finished the thought, her Johnson eyes blazing, but she looked worried again.

Daddy saw that and moved to reassure. "Don't worry, Eva. The union will stand strong against him if he tries any shenanigans." Daddy rose to get his coat. "We'll strike if it comes to that. The UAW will support us," he finished. We were a union house through and through, and I knew that workers like Daddy had to stand up for their rights against the rich company owners. That's what Daddy said. They had to be "Union Strong" or get beat down. "Union Strong, Sweet Potato." Daddy pulled out the words again for the occasion. "We gotta be Union Strong, even in a blizzard." Daddy winked at me as he headed out the door. Mom relaxed a little in his confidence.

Bess and Blue weathered through the storm fine. "Snow

covered their house and kept 'em snug," Daddy reported later. After he knew the beagles were okay, Daddy went looking for the car. He found the Dodge in front of the Meres' house, not far from Jeanette Road. Mr. Stewart helped him wrangle it out of the ditch, and even with the two of them, it took all day.

After Daddy left, I couldn't wait to get outside, but it took some doing to get dressed. Mom insisted on extra sweaters under my coat and three pairs of socks on my feet, plus galoshes to keep them dry.

Around ten I finally stepped out into a real New World. The glare was almost blinding, and I had to keep my eyes squinted tight against the intense sunlight on the snow. When I looked around, I couldn't believe it was our yard. All the landmarks were gone. As far as I could see, the snow stretched out in all directions, even and unbroken by any bushes or fences. Our coal pile was a white mountain. The outhouse roof barely showed above the drifts blown around it. Bess and Blue's house had disappeared. Our woodpile of a shed was just another snow mountain on the landscape. I felt like I had landed on the moon.

Daddy had made a path from the back garage door around the house to the front. It was a narrow snow tunnel with sides higher than my waist and came to a stop by the front door. From there I could see his deep tracks where he had taken off through the yard, heading toward the road to search for the buried Dodge. Slow going, I guess, because the snow was well past his knees. The snowscape in the front yard was broken some by piles on either side of the road where the plow had cut through and by the elm trees still standing tall above it all—Daddy's markers in the blizzard.

I stood still. I looked out at what the "Great Thanksgiving Storm," as NBC called it, had left behind and at how everything seemed changed because of it. I looked and I began to listen. No birds sang, no animals rustled, no wind whistled. The only sound in the New World was my breathing.

"You didn't stay out long." Mom was surprised to see me. "Too cold?"

"No, just too deep to play"—which wasn't exactly true. The New World of the blizzard was just too strange to stay in for long.

Ho! Ho! Ho!

Daddy got into the shop on Wednesday, the same day we started back to school. We weren't sure the bus would run but thought it might since the plow had been by a couple more times to clear Leap Road.

At school, turkey bragging was forgotten because everyone was full of blizzard stories, and I was glad because I wouldn't have to admit to the rabbit and pheasant. I did tell Thelma and she was impressed. Her family had rabbit and squirrel. But the squirrel was puny, she said, not like the fat ones in Kentucky.

Mrs. Shaw was running behind on her bulletin boards because of the snow and had to scramble to get Santa done up and the manger scene with Mary and Joseph and baby Jesus in place. And even though we needed to catch up in our subjects because of snow days, Mrs. S. was in a festive mood and had us make red and green paper chains for the school Christmas tree in the lunchroom. Mr. Moore had promised the tree would be up by Friday, so we had to cut and paste fast to get the garlands done on time.

Miss Roberts was dithered about the time lost to the blizzard. "I just don't see how we can get the Christmas program together," she fretted, but Mrs. S. offered our class' help to paint the sets. Everyone was happy.

Mom was fretting, too, in a lighthearted way. She was concerned about Christmas shopping. "First time in a long time we've had any extra for presents." Her voice was bright. "I've got to get downtown." Daddy's job at the shop was steady, with lots of overtime, so there was a little room to breathe about money. I began dreaming of a cowgirl outfit— one with a skirt and vest, a neckerchief tied under the chin, and six-shooters on the hip—one like Dale Evans wore.

Roy Rogers was the King of the Cowboys, and I never missed his radio show on Sunday nights. When eight o'clock came, I'd stop whatever I was doing to tune in the Philco and flop on the davenport for half an hour in the Old West, where people rode in stagecoaches, carried six-shooters, and organized a posse to go after cattle rustlers. Roy had a ranch out west, and he rode a Palomino horse named Trigger who could walk on his hind legs. Really. He was a horse that could do lots of tricks, and Roy took him around the country to show him off. Roy also had his amazing dog, Bullitt. Bullitt was on the Sunday show and could probably do tricks, too, but he mostly helped solve mysteries and save people in trouble and catch cattle rustlers when it was called for. Gabby was Roy's sidekick (cowboys always had sidekicks), and he talked in a gravelly voice and got the posse together when Roy needed one. Roy, Trigger, Bullitt, and Gabby—I loved them all, but my favorite on the show was Dale. Dale Evans was the Queen of the West, and I wanted to be like her.

Dale did things. That's what I liked about her. She rode fast horses, chased stagecoach robbers, pulled her six-shooter if called for, and put rustlers behind bars when she caught them. The women I knew washed clothes and fixed supper and sometimes taught school, but they never did the things that the Queen of the West could do. I wanted to be like Dale Evans.

Or like Annie Oakley or Calamity Jane. Dale Evans was on a made-up radio show, but Annie Oakley was a real sharpshooter with Buffalo Bill's Wild West Show, and Calamity Jane was a real cowgirl who could ride and shoot better than most men, even Wild Bill Hickok, who was famous. Daddy said that Annie Oakley was from Ohio, so that was one point in favor of my new state, but she wasn't alive anymore. Of course, neither was Calamity Jane, but when she was, she had lots of adventures on the trail. Sometimes I played made-up stories that I was a cowgirl who had adventures. I rode my pretend horse and made pretend campfires out on the range.

I hunted down bank robbers and outsmarted cattle thieves. A cowgirl outfit for Christmas would be perfect.

"I'm taking the bus downtown this morning," Mom told us at breakfast, "and I might not get back by the time you get home from school." I knew she was headed to the F. & R. Lazarus department store that stood on the corner of Town and High. Lazarus had six floors of merchandise, a basement (where the bargains were), and an annex on Front Street that sold big things like stoves and washers.

"Have you seen the Lazarus window this year?" Connie asked me on Monday while we were on the floor painting scenery for the music program. "Everything moves, even the elves. They've got dancing fairies that twirl around Santa's house, and Santa pops out to say 'Ho! Ho! Ho!'" Connie enthused.

The Lazarus Christmas window was a tradition, and the store unveiled the creation on the day after Thanksgiving every year. The blizzard had delayed things a day or two, but Connie confirmed that the spectacular window was operating. It was my first Ohio Christmas, so I had yet to see the Lazarus display, but school friends described it as a Christmas winter wonderland with lots of moving parts—trains rounding curves, reindeer jumping fences, lights twinkling, snow falling—all of it. The display started on the High Street side and wrapped around the building to show in the Town Street window as well. Every year people came from all over

Ohio just to see what Lazarus had come up with in their window. I wanted to be one of them.

"No, not today, Carol," Mom replied to my plea, "you have school and I am going to shop for Christmas." That was the end of it for the moment. I was disappointed, but the idea that Mom was shopping for Christmas thrilled me. I waited by the door that evening when the Hilliard bus dropped Mom off by the vulture mailbox. She was carrying Lazarus shopping bags in both hands. The special white Christmas bags were ablaze with big red and green balls, and "Merry Christmas," scrawled in sparkly red cursive, curled from the front of the bag to the back. I knew each shopping bag held lots of smaller bags with presents inside. I was excited.

But my excitement went nowhere. "Carol!" Mom was surprised to see me. "You need to go upstairs while I put some things away." She wrestled the shopping bags to make sure no secrets peeked out. When she called me back downstairs, it was to help with supper. She had changed into her housedress, tied her apron, and stood at the kitchen sink like nothing was new. No amount of questions could move her. She liked to keep her secrets.

December slid like a snail toward the big day. Mr. Moore brought in the Christmas tree for the lunchroom as promised, and besides the red and green paper garlands we had made, Third Grade strung long threads of popcorn for the tree, Second Grade hung handmade angels from top to bottom, and First Grade made pine cone reindeer to stand on the cotton snow skirt that circled the tree's trunk. Mrs. Shaw's room sparkled Christmas in every possible corner, and even the Triple M hung a wreath on her classroom door. Miss Roberts loved the scenery we painted but was soon fretting about the costumes for the program. She was especially troubled by the sheep. Shepherds were easy—bathrobes and towels—but sheep were a different challenge. Mrs. S. came to the rescue: white woolly shirts dotted with cotton balls. She added a pillowcase head that completed the look, and Miss Roberts was satisfied.

After the costumes and scenery got settled, Miss Roberts started rehearsals. The program was for an all-school performance on the Friday before Christmas vacation. I was in the choir and had no speaking part, but the choir was required at all the practices. Miss Roberts liked perfection and drilled the actors with multiple run-throughs. Mary and Joseph traveled across the school stage to Bethlehem. The brown blanket donkey followed beside them, powered by two bent-over third graders shuffling along inside. Angels with cardboard wings pinned to their backs were "heard on high" while bathrobe shepherds and cotton-ball sheep made their way to the box-of-straw manger in the center of the stage. Baby Jesus got born over and over at Hilliard School in the weeks before Christmas.

Uptown Hilliard got in the Christmas spirit too. We

watched the day-to-day transformation from the school bus windows. Oddly, Mr. Turney's Pool Hall and Sparkey's Beer Bar next door were the first out with door wreaths. Sparkey's missed the Halloween paint-up but would not be left behind at Christmas. Winterringer's was decked out the following day with red-bowed greenery in the two front windows, and Clyde Adkins decorated his sign with green ribbon wrapped around his red-and-white barber pole. It was a festive inside barber joke, no doubt. Both grocery stores had Scots pine trees for sale, wrapped tightly with hairy twine and lined up like dead bodies against their front windows. I knew Daddy would not get our tree until Christmas Eve, when stores were trying to unload the last scraggly remains. It was part of his "get a good deal" strategy.

I was particularly curious to see any decorations that went up in the Ginny's Beauty Shop window. I still didn't know who was responsible for the Halloween wash-down that ended my brief artist career, but I had come to secretly blame Ginny. The thing I couldn't figure was why.

I got a hint the morning we spotted a raggedy tinfoil Christmas tree listing to the right in her front window. "Now ain't that ugly?" Thelma summed up the common opinion on the bus. The dreadful artificial contraption that Ginny chose as her shop's Christmas decoration was an affront to the pine-scented sprays of fresh greenery that decked out McMillian's Hardware a block away, and even to Clyde's green-ribbon barber pole. "She might know haircuts," Thelma went on, "but she ain't got no sense 'bout what looks good in 'er wind'a." There it was. No wonder Ginny had washed off my witch masterpiece. She just didn't appreciate how good it was. Right then I decided to forgive her for the Halloween embarrassment. It was Christmas after all—the goodwill-to-men time of the year. Ginny wasn't in the "men" category, but I extended the spirit of the season to cover her.

Mom did know what looked good, and she was no slacker in the Christmas decoration department. I came home one day in mid-December ready to stretch out and solve mysteries with Nancy Drew, only to find that Mom had a job for me. "Keep your coat on, Carol." She met me at the door with a butcher knife in her hand. "I need your help to get some greens." We headed back to the fence where there was a gigantic evergreen bush. "I want to cut some of this juniper to make a wreath." She nodded toward the bush that took up a whole corner of the yard. "You bunch up the branches and hold them so I can get to the stems with the knife." She showed me where to put my hands to stay away from her cuts.

It took close to an hour to get all the greenery Mom needed. She had big plans. "I want to make wreaths for both doors and a grave blanket for the cemetery." Mom said that last part as if it were just another Christmas decoration like the door wreaths, but I knew it wasn't. The grave blanket was for Norma's grave. When my sister Norma got sick and died, it was right at Christmastime. That was a fact of our family. And even though they never mentioned it, Christmas carried a lot of really bad memories for Mom and Daddy. Norma died before I was born, so I never knew her, but I did know about the sadness her death left behind.

Over time I had begun to understand that Mom and Daddy did different things about their sadness. Daddy spent time at Sparkey's Beer Bar and came home blurry-eyed and all talky, like he didn't have a care. Maybe the beer did stop the hurt for a while—I didn't know. But I did know it made Mom mad, as I had seen again at Thanksgiving, so trips to Sparkey's brought other problems into our house.

Mom had a different approach. She took her sadness with her into a deep, dark place inside, and when that happened, it was like she went away from us. She would "take to her bed," as Daddy called it, in the middle of the day and do and say only what she had to. Her eyes would be flat and dull, as if the light had blown out inside. I had learned I could do nothing to make her sad mood go away. I could only wait until her inside light came back on.

Sometimes instead of taking to her bed, Mom did the opposite to push her sadness aside or at least delay it for a while. She'd keep busy. And I mean *busy*. The "keep busy" approach was in full force as the Christmas anniversary of Norma's death neared.

"I can't get this wreath right." Mom futzed with the juniper for almost a whole day. She wired and rewired this branch, then that as she tried for the look she wanted. She trimmed and shaped tiny twigs with the scissors and did and redid the big red bows. "There, that's the best I can do." She slapped down the scissors, still not satisfied with the two massive door wreaths she had fashioned, complete with snazzy wide-ribbon red bows. "Help me get 'em hung, Carol." She was resigned to the imperfection. We hung the wreaths, and I thought they were stunning.

"They're the best on Leap Road." I stood back for a view. "Even better than the ones at McMillian's Hardware." And I meant it. Mom just frowned and fussed, then went inside to start the grave blanket for Norma's headstone.

It took all of an afternoon to finish the wreath for Norma's grave, but it, too, was "not right" even though Mom had created a long, elegant spray of greenery intertwined with somber, dark-red ribbon. She instructed Daddy to lay it on Norma's cemetery marker the next day on the way home from the shop. "It's shabby," she concluded, "but I can't do any better."

The greenery done, Mom started in on other decorations to keep busy. Christmas cards were first. We had at least fifty already, and more arrived in the vulture mailbox every day. All Mom's and Daddy's relatives sent cards, including some cousins I had never heard of. Friends from the shop sent Christmas greetings, and so did neighbors who lived on Leap Road. I never saw the sense in that. We could just knock on their doors and say "Merry Christmas," but that was not how people did. Christmas cards were an important part of the season.

Daddy didn't like to spend money, even at Christmas, but Mom did what she did regardless. In honor of Mom's shopping, F. & R. Lazarus sent the Richardsons a special holiday card in an oversized red envelop closed with a round gold seal on the back flap. "You must be big friends with Fred and Robert," Daddy chided, "if they're sending us such a fancy Christmas card." Fred and Robert were the F and R in F. & R. Lazarus.

Mom sorted the cards by color and size, then taped each one individually around the windows in the front room. She worked on the project while we were in school and surprised us with her designs. The best was a triangle Christmas tree made of cards and curled ribbon that covered the wall behind the davenport. It made even the dreary painted pasteboard look festive.

The last week before Christmas, Mom stopped her downtown shopping trips, so I guessed that all the presents were bought. "I'll take the trash out," I offered unexpectedly one afternoon. Mom was surprised by my sudden interest in trash, maybe even suspicious, but said nothing. Day after day I carried out the wastebasket without being asked and dutifully took it to the burn barrel across from the outhouse. But before I dumped it, I rummaged thoroughly for signs that Mom had bought the cowgirl outfit I so hoped for. Maybe she had discarded the Lazarus receipt that listed it. Or better, maybe she had trashed the telltale box—the one that surely pictured a happy girl my age with a lasso in one hand and a six-shooter in the other. I searched the trash for a week but found nothing "cowgirl." I did see scraps of Christmas paper, so at least Mom was wrapping something. I just didn't have a clue what it might be.

With the shopping done, the wreaths on the door, and the cards on the windows and wall, Mom turned to candy making. She started with cocoa fudge, which took a long time to make and was difficult to get just right. After breakfast on Saturday, Mom mixed sugar and Hershey's cocoa powder with water and put it on to boil in a heavy pot. "You gotta watch it close," she instructed, "or it'll turn grainy. Tell me when it gets to a rolling boil."

After it had "rolled" for a while, Mom drizzled a few drops of the glossy brown mixture into a small bowl of cold water. "Test it like this, Carol." She gently swirled the water with her two fingers. "It needs to get to the soft ball stage." Mom showed me the marble of chocolate candy that had formed in the cold water. "That's good, I think." She turned off the flame and moved the pot to a cold burner. "Put in the butter and the vanilla," she nodded to me, "but don't stir it. It's gotta cool first."

Mom had the second batch going while the first pot cooled. "We'll put nuts in this one," she explained and set me to shelling walnuts into a measuring cup. "Don't leave any shells," she warned, but I already knew. Nothing ruined a fudge bite more than a stray shell.

The cooled batch was ready to beat, and Mom took it on with her wooden spoon. I cracked nuts and watched for the rolling boil on batch number two while Mom poured and spread the thick, glossy fudge from batch one into a square pan to set.

"Here, give this a try." She handed me a dark-brown chunk on her scoring knife and took a taste for herself. The rich chocolate candy melted warm and creamy on my tongue.

I closed my eyes to the deliciousness. "Mmmmm!"

"Not right," Mom pronounced as she smacked her lips and tested the fudge's texture with her tongue against the roof of her mouth. "Not right," she repeated. "Too grainy. You feel that?" I did not. I thought it was perfect.

"Hand me the cocoa. I'll start another batch." And so it went for batch after batch the rest of the day. By the time Daddy got home, the sweet smell of chocolate and vanilla filled every nook, and plates of dark, glossy fudge lined the kitchen counter and took over the big dinner table in the front room. We had no idea what to do with the pounds of finished fudge—some with nuts and some without, and none "right"—but the important thing was accomplished: Mom had kept busy the entire day.

The next morning, Mom protested but helped me pack five tins of fudge to take to school—one each for Mrs. S., Miss Roberts, and Mr. Moore, a big one for the women who cooked for us in the lunchroom, and a really big one to share with the rest of the class. "I don't know why you'd take this ole stuff to school," Mom mumbled as she chose the best-cut pieces to fill the tins. "Nobody's gonna want to eat it." But of course they did. The class tin was down to crumbs and tiny chocolate slivers when I brought it home at the end of the day. "They're kids." Mom dismissed the empty tin. "They don't know what good fudge oughta be." She didn't much believe in compliments.

But Mom did believe in invitations, and she had already said yes to Mrs. Murdock, who wanted us to come to her house the Saturday before Christmas to see the Christ in the cradle.

"Christ in the cradle?" I was suspicious. I had visions of yet another situation where the baby Jesus got born over and over again. I'd seen enough of that for one year.

"It's a flower." I was surprised by Mom's answer. "Mrs. Murdock has one, and she wants us to see it." So after supper on Saturday, Mom, Jerry, and I crawled through the hole in the fence and headed across Mrs. Murdock's yard. We didn't have to knock because Mrs. Murdock flung open the door before we got to it.

"Merry Christmas! Come in! Come in!" She hustled us into her kitchen. We barely fit. Mrs. Murdock's house had one door to the outside and three rooms inside—a kitchen, front room, and bedroom. All were exceedingly small and stuffed with furniture. "Sit down! Sit down!" We shuffled en masse into the front room. Mrs. Murdock loved company, and she beamed over us as we took seats on the edge of a davenport laced with doilies across the back. "Please pass the cookies, Jerry. They're on the table there." Mrs. Murdock was eager to get the festivities started. She was a jolly sort, with her curly white hair and red cheeks looking like she had just come in from the cold. She reminded me of Mrs. Claus if Santa had a Mrs.

We crunched and munched our way through the plate of star-shaped cookies. I caught the sprinkles of red sugar in my open hand so they would not spoil the white davenport, but after the third cookie my palm turned Christmas red from melted sugar. "May I be excused?" I asked as I sidestepped my way around a lamp on the way to the kitchen sink. "I need to wash my hands." Mom and Mrs. Murdock nodded and kept chatting.

From the kitchen, I half listened to blizzard stories and gossip about the neighbors—whose machine got stuck in a drift, whose roof took a leak but, "thank God," didn't fall in, whose baby was born without help "because ole Doc Carr couldn't get through." The stories wound around and circled back to start over. I lost interest. Where was the Christ in the cradle? I glanced around the kitchen and into the front room.

I spotted it off to the side in a dark corner, wedged between two fat chairs. Right away I recognized what it was. One exactly like it sat for sale in the window of Conklin's furniture store. I looked toward Jerry. He had seen it too. And in a flash we both knew that Mrs. Murdock hadn't invited us over to see the Christ in the cradle. She invited us to see her new television set!

"Is that yours?" I interrupted the story telling. "Is that your television set?" I breathed out the question in amazement.

"I wondered when you were going to notice." Mrs. Murdock was pleased. Mom too. She was in on the trick. "From Conklin's"—pride in the words—"Philco ten-inch Bakelite. Just got it delivered today." The brown television set perched on a swivel table like a one-eyed bird watching us. The "eye" was a squashed glass circle—round on each side and flat on the top and bottom.

"Let's turn it on and see if we can get something." Mrs. Murdock reached for the knob. I was about to see my first television show ever!

As it turned out, we did watch the Christ in the cradle bloom that night at Mrs. Murdock's. It was a glorious white blossom that opened slowly during the evening and by midnight showed the insides that did, if you looked carefully and used your imagination, resemble baby Jesus on a manger of golden straw. And the sweet fragrance of the flower took over the entire house, just like Mrs. Murdock had said it would.

While we waited for the blooming, we watched ring-side wrestling on Mrs. Murdock's new Philco television. On the ten-inch screen, two big, muscly men in tiny, tight shorts strutted around a square-roped "ring." They pranced from corner to corner, grunted, sweated till they glistened, and tried to get the "hammerlock hold" on the other muscly guy. The hammerlock hold meant squeezing the opponent's head until he couldn't stand it anymore and cried "uncle," or whatever, to say he gave up. Tag-team matches were really fun too. Two big guys in the tiny, tight shorts danced around in the ring, grunting and sweating and trying hammerlocks while two other big guys in tiny shorts stayed outside the roped square, each waiting to get tagged by his partner so he could jump into the ring to grunt, sweat, and try hammerlocks. It was wonderful. Jumping Jim Brunzell was my favorite wrestler, and Gorgeous George was the star everyone adored. In one short night, I learned to love television.

Daddy surprised us the next morning when we came down for breakfast. It was Sunday, and we expected him to be at the shop just like every other day. "Only working half a day and it's the second half," he explained, "because it's Christmas Eve and we gotta get a tree in here." He twinkled on, "Santa'll want to know where to leave all those pieces of coal he's been savin' up for you two."

"Oh, Daddy, Santa doesn't leave coal," I objected.

"Depends on how good you've been," he countered.

"You probably got nothing to worry about, Sweet Potato, but guess we'll know in the morning." The final tease.

Over breakfast, we told Daddy all about the hammer-locks, the dinky shorts, and of course the ten-inch Philco television from Conklin's Furniture Store that now sat in Mrs. Murdock's house. He was sorry he had missed it all, but he'd had to work late to make up for the time he would lose on his half-day Sunday.

"Can we get the tree now?" Jerry wanted to know. He was as excited as I was.

"Layin' in the garage already." Daddy had kept his surprise until after breakfast. "Went up to Huffman's IGA and picked it out this morning before you sleepyheads got up. They were selling 'em cheap—tryin' to get rid of 'em," he clucked like he did when he made a good deal. Mom looked away. She figured the tree would be a scraggly leftover, but she swallowed her "you get what you pay for" line. "Jerry, let's go get it on a stand." Daddy pushed back from the table. "Carol, you help your mother fix a place in the front room."

Mom and I shoved the gray armchair over to make a spot in front of the window. "Lights'll shine to the outside," said Mom the decorator. "And we don't want to put it too close to the stove. Heat'd dry it out—might even catch on fire." We could hear Daddy and Jerry nailing the wooden X to the bottom of the tree so it would stand. Finally they came, carrying it in through the front door, and set it in place.

"Let's cut the strings and see how she looks." Daddy pulled out his pocketknife. The twine fell to the floor, and we fluffed out the imprisoned branches. It was a Scots pine with long needles, gnarly branches going every which way, and lots of bare spots.

"Turn the bad spots toward the window so they won't show," Mom directed. "Put the best side out." Daddy rotated the tree this way and that while Mom looked on. "Not right." She rejected each turn and finally gave up. "Just put the lights on." Daddy started at the top and circled the tree to the bottom with red, green, blue, and yellow bulbs. The tree looked better with color.

"Let's hang this one in a special place." Mom handed me a red glass ball striped with white rings. I found a branch in the middle and went back for the next ornament. We draped the branches with shiny foil icicles as a final touch and stood back to look it over.

"Not bad," Daddy appraised, "and such a good deal."

Mom shook her head at the last part, but we all agreed that the tree turned out better than we had ever thought it might. "Glass balls and a few lights can make even a sow's ear shine." Mom's final word on the Christmas tree.

"Where are the stockings?" Jerry wanted to know.

"And the cookies for Santa?" I put in. "If we don't have cookies out, he might pass right over." I had some serious doubts about the Santa thing—old man in a red suit flying all over the world in a sled pulled by eight reindeer to de-liver just-what-you-want-most presents to every kid, really? But I kept my suspicions to myself. "He might not know we moved." I played along instead.

"Santa knows; he keeps a list." Mom picked up the game. "And I baked a double batch of his favorite cookies yesterday—Nestlé Toll House with plenty of chocolate chips." I knew they were Mom's favorite too.

After Daddy left for the shop, we spent the rest of the day getting everything just right. Jerry started with the stockings. We didn't have a chimney, so he tacked them in a prominent place by the window next to the tree—a place even an old man tired from an around-the-world trip couldn't miss. Mom fut-zed with a table decoration for Christmas dinner and put me to work shelling hickory nuts. We had collected the nuts from the tree out back and saved them for a special cake Mom often made at Christmas. The hickory nuts were small, and the meat hard to pick out, but I thought they were the best—except for Brazil nuts, which I sometimes got in my stocking. While we worked, we listened to Christmas carols on the radio and sang along with the familiar tunes. "I'm dreaming of a white Christ-mas," Mom crooned with Bing Crosby. Daddy would get home late, so we ate a cold sandwich supper. Of course, Mom would make a big dinner for Christmas Day.

Since none of my pre-Christmas detective work had produced evidence of the hoped-for cowgirl outfit, I was ready to give up and leave it all to Santa Claus, the guy I had so many doubts about. Then Mom had another job for me that changed my mind about giving up. She wanted mistletoe hung from the bare rafter in the middle of the front-room ceiling. While I was standing on the chair, looking for the perfect mistletoe place, I spotted something else. Right then I vowed to play sleuth one last time. My new plan depended on a secret hidden under my bed.

After dark, we settled around the Philco for the NBC Christmas Special. It turned out to be a show called "Santa Claus Is No Saint" with Vincent Price, who played a gumshoe detective. We were all surprised at a detective program on Christmas Eve—we were expecting angels or the three kings on camels who followed the star to Bethlehem. But I thought a Christmas Eve detective show was kind of ironic considering my plan, and I took it as a sign that I was on the right track. "I'm going to bed," I announced when the show was over. Mom was surprised. "The sooner I get to sleep, the sooner Santa will come." I stretched and yawned. "Besides, I'm tired." I wasn't really, but pretending to be sleepy and going to bed early was part one of my strategy. Jerry surprised me by heading to bed too. My plan was in motion.

We settled into our rooms upstairs, and pretty soon I heard Jerry's sleep-breathing coming through the thin pasteboard wall. I stared into the dark. Waiting. Downstairs all was quiet except for the Christmas music on the radio. Then:

"Carol, Carol," Mom almost whispered at the bottom of the stairs, "are you awake?" Silence. "Are you awake?" she said a second time, louder to be sure. I hardly breathed. Satisfied, Mom closed the pasteboard door at the bottom of the stairs.

Rustle. Crackle. Scrunch. I heard new sounds. Mom was up to something. I sprang into action. Well, not exactly *sprang*. I eased out of my bed to the bare wood floor. Careful to make no sound, I dropped to my hands and knees and inched forward under the bed. My fingers played over the floor to find the knothole I knew was there. I had first discovered it one boring summer afternoon and had seen it again while I hung mistletoe.

"Ah! There it is," I mouthed silently. I put my spy-eye over the hole. It gave a clear view of the entire front room—just what I needed. Right away I spotted Mom next to the Christmas tree. F. & R. Lazarus bags dangled from both hands. She set them down and started to work. "Santa Claus," I murmured, my suspicions confirmed. I wasn't sure I was glad or sad at the discovery. By the time Mom/Santa finished, the shopping bags were limp and stacks of wrapped Christmas packages nested under the tree. Mama Claus took the empty shopping bags and disappeared into the kitchen. On the way, she lifted a Nestlé Toll House chocolate-chip cookie off Santa's plate and slipped it into her mouth. I guess she was entitled.

Nothing came into my spy-eye view for some time, but I heard the back door open, then close. Finally Mom reappeared. She had a gun—a BB gun. *Exactly what Jerry wanted*, I thought as I watched her prop Jerry's gun next to the tree where he would be sure to see it first on Christmas morning. In my family, unwrapped gifts always came directly from Santa and they were the most special. My heart picked up a beat. Expectantly I waited for Mom to leave the room and return with the exactly-what-I-wanted cowgirl outfit. But Mom surprised me. She sat down on the davenport and reached for the cookie plate. Her Santa job was finished. When the cookies were gone, she turned out the light and went to bed.

Reluctantly I crawled back under the covers. My detective work uncovered two things: there was no jolly, red-suited Santa Claus, and there was no cowgirl outfit for me.

I woke Christmas morning to Jerry's whooping and hollering. "I can't believe Santa got the BB gun! It's exactly what I wanted!" I heard him cocking the gun and shooting air out of the barrel. He was so happy. After last night's detecting fiasco, I resolved to like whatever was under the tree with my name on it, even though it wasn't what I wanted most. I put on a smiley face and headed for the stairs.

"There she is!" Daddy was standing in front of the lighted tree. "Merry Christmas, sleepyhead. Ole Santa may have left you more than lumps of coal. Come look." And with that, he stepped to the right so I could see what was behind him under the tree. "I think it's exactly what you wanted," he said, beaming.

You guessed it. It was the cowgirl outfit—hat, boots, a vest with fringe, and a two-holster set of six-shooters—all of it. Just like Dale Evans. But who put it there, right where I would see it as soon as I came downstairs? Not Daddy. He worked the four-to-midnight shift. Not Mom. She ate all the cookies and went to bed. I saw everything through the knot-hole—Santa/Mom in the middle of the night with F. & R. Lazarus bags, a BB gun, and no cowgirl outfit.

I was stunned. "Aren't you going to try it on?" Mom urged.

"But, but, I saw . . . I didn't . . . I didn't think Santa got it" was all I could say. Mom and Daddy exchanged a twinkly, Santa Clausy kind of wink. I got tricked, but I never learned how.

"Ho! Ho! Ho!" Daddy headed to his favorite chair to enjoy the rest of Christmas day.

Winter Surprises

The weather held through Christmas vacation with no unexpected blizzards, and Jerry got to take his new BB gun to the field. "Don't shoot at anything you don't plan to kill," Daddy warned, "or wound an animal and leave it to suffer." I secretly hoped Jerry was a bad shot and wouldn't hit anything. What was the point of killing a sparrow or even a bigger blue jay? Neither one was any size to eat. Killing just to kill didn't make sense to me.

But I had my guns too. They couldn't really shoot, but I wore them slung on my hip every day as part of my new cowgirl outfit. When I slid the boots on my feet and strapped the six-shooters to my waist, I was Calamity Jane or sometimes Annie Oakley or even Dale Evans. "You're gonna wear those out in a week," Mom teased when I came down for breakfast with guns blazing again. But the day after New Year's, I laid them aside and appeared at the table dressed for school. Christmas vacation was over, and the long march of winter began again.

On the bus, Thelma wanted to know if I had gotten the cowgirl outfit, and she was as stumped as I was about how it got under the tree. "Might be ta' real Santy," she offered, "an' he snuck in after your ma went ta' bed." I shrugged a maybe. "But if 'twas, he forgot ta' stop by our place." Thelma was skeptical again. The Rigsby family had a poor Christmas, she explained. Her daddy had gotten laid off right before. "Boss just up an' said, 'Ain't no work. Go home.' An' that was ta' end of hit."

"He should join the union," I posed. "Workers got to stand together to protect their jobs. That's what my daddy says."

"They ain't got no union thar," Thelma finished. "We jus' keep hopin' things'll pick up." There was nothing more to say.

"Surprise came in the mail today." Mom greeted me when I got home from school. She beamed anticipation at the pasteboard box sitting on the cedar chest. "It's from Irene and Uncle Vinson," she said, but I had already guessed. Irene and Uncle Vinson were my aunt and uncle in Maryland. Irene was a sister in the Johnson Clan, and one of Mom's favorites. "We'll wait till everyone's home to see inside." I could hardly wait. Presents from Irene and Uncle Vinson were a second Christmas.

When we opened the package after supper, Jerry got a tackle box that starred a fold out tray filled with rubber worms and hand-painted fish lures dangling hooks from their sides. A spinner fishing reel was tucked in the bottom section. Jerry was tickled. "Guess Uncle Vinson knows what you like," Daddy put in. Uncle Vinson was a fisherman on Solomons Island and a charter-boat captain on the Chesapeake Bay. The bay was where Daddy's gift had come from.

"Vinson never lets me down at Christmas." Daddy held up his prized can of fresh Maryland oysters. "Eva, if I get you some cream, think you could make me some of your oyster stew?" Fresh oysters from Uncle Vinson made Christmas for Daddy.

Mom got a set of fancy bed sheets. The bottom one was pastel yellow, and the top one was white sprinkled all over with tiny yellow flowers. The top end was lacy, so it would be an elegant fold-down when the bed was made up. The pillowcases were lacy, too, and matched the fold-down on the top sheet. "These are too pretty to use for every day." Mom ran her fingers over the luxurious linen. "We'll save 'em for company," she decided. She liked to hold back her best for visitors.

My gift was a dress with pale lavender flowers and delicate lace that striped the front from shoulders to hem. I'd never had a dress so fine and so beautiful that it took my breath away. But that's not why I remember it so well. I remember it because that beautiful dress and what came after almost took Mom away for good.

"I want to try it on!" I held the dress against my front to check the size. The fabric was gauzy thin, like a damselfly wing. "Can I put it on now?" I felt like a princess and spun around to the mirror to admire how I looked. Mom dropped her eyes away. Silent. Daddy sagged like a popped balloon. They exchanged a glance that I caught in the mirror's reflection.

"In a minute, Sweet Potato." Daddy spoke softly in a way that warned me away from my enthusiasm. Then to Mom, even softer, "It'll be okay, Eva," and finally, "Take the dress upstairs, Carol, and try it on. Come down when you're ready." When I returned, I could tell Daddy and Mom had come to a decision while I was gone. They oohed and aahed at how nice I looked in the beautiful dress, like you'd expect, but the light was gone from their eyes. When I changed to my old clothes, like Cinderella after the ball, Mom took the dress to "put it away for something special." I never saw it again.

Mom didn't get up to fix our breakfast the next morning. And she was still in bed when we got home from school. I went into the darkened front bedroom, and I could see the long, motionless form of her body under the covers. "Mom, are you all right?" I spoke into the silence. "Mom?"

"I'm okay." She turned to her other side but kept her head covered.

"Should I start supper?" I wanted her to talk to me.

"What should I fix?" I tried again for a response.

"Whatever you want." Even that much effort exhausted her. I knew she had gone to the dark place inside her where nothing outside mattered. I left her there and tried to figure out what we could eat for supper.

Even Daddy couldn't rouse Mom when he got home. "You need to get up a little, Eva," he encouraged, but she refused.

"I'll try tomorrow" was her best offer, but Mom stayed in her dark place. Every morning, I came downstairs hoping to find her in the kitchen cooking breakfast, but morning after morning the long, motionless form under the covers was all that greeted me.

"When is Mom coming back?" I finally asked Daddy one night over supper.

"Soon, Sweet Potato" was all he offered. I could see the worry in his eyes.

"Why did she take to her bed?" I had worked the question in my mind and come to my own conclusions. "Was it the dress?" Daddy looked up sharply, surprised.

"Maybe." His answer was careful, like stepping around a fresh cow patty. "That's what got it started, I think. But it's that time of year," he finished with a resigned shrug. He left me to fill in for myself the part about Norma's dying at Christmastime.

"But why the dress?" I persisted.

Daddy thought a long time before he answered. "Norma had one almost like it." His voice dragged through his own sadness. In a flash I remembered the photo in the Picture Box—Norma glancing wistfully over her shoulder, walking away in a pale lacy dress striped with delicate flowers—the same dress Mom still kept neat and folded in the cedar chest.

Mom's dark days went on deep into January's gray bitterness. She stayed in bed, rarely spoke more than a few words, and hardly ate even though we coaxed her with things she usually liked. Then the coughing began. Somehow Mom got a cold that turned into pleurisy in her chest. All the way upstairs, I could hear her hacking spasms during the night and the accompanying groans of pain. "I'm getting Doc Carr out here," Daddy insisted against Mom's protests, and he headed to town to get the doctor. Doc Carr followed the Dodge to Leap Road and parked his car in the drive behind Daddy. He carried his black leather doctor bag into the room where Mom was.

"You need to sit up, Mrs. Richardson," he directed, all business. "I want to check what's going on inside." Dr. Carr took a long time to listen to Mom's chest. He thumped in front and then in back while he concentrated on the sound coming from Mom's lungs through his stethoscope.

"Well, I don't hear any pneumonia," he pronounced as he hung his stethoscope around his neck. "At least not yet," he added. "I'm going to tape up your chest to help the pleurisy."

He brought out a roll of white adhesive tape from his bag. "And I'm going to give you some codeine syrup to get that cough under control and some pain pills that will help you rest." He pulled out special scissors to cut the tape. *Rest?* I wondered. All Mom did these days was rest.

Dr. Carr wound the tape tight round and round Mom's chest so her insides wouldn't rub together when she coughed. "That's what's causing the pain," he explained. Didn't make sense to me, but the tape must have worked because Mom did breathe easier when he was done. Then Dr. Carr pulled two bottles out of his bag—one was the codeine syrup for Mom's cough and the other held the little white pain pills to help her "rest."

"Take a teaspoon of the syrup every four hours," he directed, "and one of the pills with a glass of water. Let's get you dosed up before I leave."

"Carol, bring some water and a spoon from the kitchen." Daddy waited on the other side of the bed while I filled a glass from the spigot and fetched a teaspoon from the silverware drawer. By the time Dr. Carr pulled out to drive back to town, Mom was curled back under the covers. We had a quiet night.

I hoped that Mom would feel better enough in the morning to get up, but I was disappointed. And disappointed again to find her still huddled under the covers when I got home from school. She stayed huddled the next day and the next.

The bottles of medicine from Dr. Carr sat on the table by Mom's bed, and each day there was less codeine syrup and fewer and fewer pain pills. Dr. Carr brought a new supply when she ran out. Her cough went away, but day by day she went deeper into her dark place. She either slept or stared at the ceiling—that was all. As the days passed, I could tell that Mom was slipping further and further away from us. I wanted to tell Daddy about my worries, but he was working double shifts on a big General Motors job at the shop. He left early before I got up and came home late every night.

I walked into the house one afternoon, and the first thing I noticed was the silence. It was Friday and warm for January. Jerry had taken off on his bike after the school bus had dropped us off by the vulture mailbox, and I had gone up to the house. I could feel something was wrong as soon as I stepped inside.

"Mom? Mom?" My call was a question to the silence. I moved into the bedroom where she lay. "Mom?" No answer. I leaned my ear close and was relieved to hear her breathing. But her breath was wrong—it was too quiet and too deep and it really scared me. I tried again to rouse her and finally got a faint "I'm okay," but she wasn't.

I stood still as stone. I needed to do something, but what? My eyes searched the room for help, and I spotted the bottles on the bedside table—the codeine syrup and the pills to make Mom "rest." And in an instant I knew: I had to get the medicine bottles out of Mom's reach before it was too late. Without hesitating, I swept them off the table into my dress pocket. Both bottles were almost empty and I knew they shouldn't have been.

The next morning, Mom was groggy, but she talked a little and wanted some dry toast to settle her stomach. "Where is my medicine?" She glanced at the empty bedside table.

"Must be all gone," I sidestepped. Mom gave me a curious look but said no more. Over the next week, Mom got better and slowly came back to us from her darkness. She never mentioned the bottles of medicine again, and I never asked about my lacy dress with lavender flowers.

◆◆◆

January finally ended and brought a February full of surprises. The first one came on the first Saturday. As soon as I came downstairs, I knew something was up because the big, round metal bathtub was full of water and set on the floor behind the bedroom stove to stay warm. Sunday was bath day, not Saturday, and always in the evening, not the morning. So, yep, something was up.

Mom told me what it was as soon as I hit the kitchen. "Hurry up, Carol! We need to shake the stink off." That made me smile. When Mom said "shake the stink off," she didn't mean to shake out a rug or anything like that. She meant to shake off the old stuff that was bothering you and go have some fun. After the hard January, we definitely needed some laughs. "We're taking the eleven o'clock bus. Eat your breakfast and get a bath. The water's almost warm enough, and I've got some boiling to pour in when you're ready." I caught her excitement and gobbled my toast in four bites. I didn't yet know what fun we would be shaking up, but I did know the stink of January was fading.

With the toast plate and milk glass in the sink to be washed up with the supper dishes, I headed straight for the tub. I got firsts in the water and Mom took seconds. Even though we didn't have to haul water from outside anymore, it was still a sizable job to tote bucket after bucket from the kitchen to the galvanized washtub in the bedroom behind the stove. And we had to heat the bathwater on the kitchen cookstove first. All that work to fill and warm bathwater meant two things: we only took baths once a week (with "sponge baths" in between), and three people used the same water. Daddy took a shower at the shop every day, or it would have been four. So being first in the tub was big because that person got the fresh water.

"Your turn," I called out to Mom while I was drying off. We still had plenty of time, but I was excited. The bus ran from Hilliard to downtown Columbus three times a day on weekdays and Saturdays—once in the morning to get folks to work, once in the evening to get them home, and once in the middle for shoppers. We would take the shoppers' bus, which would drop us off in front of F. & R. Lazarus at noon. "Can we eat lunch downtown?" I asked in-the-tub Mom.

"Maybe," she teased, but I knew we would. I put on my best outfit because everyone got dressed up to go downtown. Everyone. Always. Mom would surely wear her mink-tail coat, which was a hand-me-down from sister Alice but not worn out at all. It was dark-red wool and cut just right to show off Mom's thin waist. Shiny, dark-brown mink tails dangled four to a side from each shoulder next to the collar. I loved to stroke the soft fur but tried not to think about the eight mink that gave up their tails—and their lives. It was a beautiful coat.

We were ready and waiting when the Hilliard bus stopped at the end of our black cinder drive. "Going down to shop, Mrs. Richardson? Good day for it. You having lunch in the Chintz Room, Carol? You're all dressed up." Joe Jollif drove the Hilliard bus, and he knew everyone who rode it. If he heard your name once, he never forgot it.

"Might shop, Mr. Jollif, might just see the sights." Mom was pleasant but revealed nothing. We each dropped a quarter in the fare box. "Evening bus run at the regular time?" she asked to change the subject. Mom wasn't much on small talk.

"I'll be on the Town Street side of Lazarus at five fifteen, just like always," he smiled.

"Don't leave without us." Mom smiled back, warming up a bit. We walked halfway back and settled in for the ride downtown. Passengers never felt a bump while riding in the fat, stuffed seats of the Hilliard bus.

"See you at five fifteen," Mr. Jollif reminded each person who stepped off in front of F. & R. Lazarus on High Street, "round the corner on the Town Street side."

Our bus unloaded passengers at the same stop as the streetcars that ran up and down High Street and across town. A long arm poked from the top of each streetcar to touch the overhead wire running high alongside the street. Sparks spit out sometimes where the arm touched the wire. "What's that?" I was alarmed the first time I saw the sparks.

"The streetcar runs on electric," Mom answered, "and sometimes the electric jumps out a little, but not enough to hurt anything." Mom and I rode the streetcar sometimes from downtown to Hudson Street up north. Daddy usually met us on the corner as he passed by on the way home from the shop at four o'clock. But not that day because he was working an overtime Saturday shift, and we needed a lot of time to shake off the stink January had left on us.

"We got to hustle a bit," Mom said, all business as soon as our feet hit the sidewalk. "Let's have lunch at Lazarus; then we have to be someplace by one thirty." She was being mysterious. "How about the Colonial Room?" She was back to lunch talk. "It's on the first floor and will be quicker."

"I love eating there!" I picked up my pace as we went through the revolving front door at Lazarus. We made our way quickly past the glass display counters of sparkling jewelry and past the escalators—one that went down to the basement bargains and one that went up to the second floor (women's dresses). We did not look at shoes on display or stop to check the new purses or flowery scarves. We did not stop until we were seated at a table in the Colonial Room restaurant.

"I'll have a bowl of bread dressing with chicken gravy," I told the waitress, "and a salad with bacon vinaigrette."

"I'll have the bread dressing too." Mom gave her order. "But with beef gravy. And," she turned to me, "let's order our dessert now so it won't take extra time."

"Chocolate cake." I didn't have to think a second. This really was a "shake off the stink" day.

"You ready?" Mom watched as I put the last crumb of Lazarus chocolate cake in my mouth. She was itching to go. "We have to walk to Broad Street." She glanced at her watch. "It's five after one." Mom paid our bill with her Lazarus charge card, and we reversed our steps past the shoes, flowery scarves, escalators, and sparkling watches and through Lazarus' revolving door onto High Street. Mom was on a mission. She didn't glance in the window at Kresge's Five and Dime or at Mills Restaurant with the turning windmill sign overhead. We just "hightailed it" (as Grandpa would say) up the sidewalk until we came to Broad Street.

We took a few steps on Broad toward the Scioto River

and stopped in front of the Palace Theater! Then I knew the "shake the stink off" surprise Mom had in mind—the marquee overhead told me everything I needed to know.

NOW SHOWING!

Walt Disney's Song of the South

"Oh, Mom!" I danced on my toes. Even I knew that *Song of the South* was about Uncle Remus and Brer Rabbit, that trickster who was always outsmarting everyone. I could tell the tar-baby and briar-patch stories without thinking.

"One adult, one child." Mom handed a dollar bill to the woman perched in the sidewalk ticket booth.

"Show's about to start." The ticket seller hurried us along. "The usher will show you to your seats." A tall young man met us in the aisle at the back of the theater. He looked very proper, dressed in a white shirt and a coat with tails and brass buttons. And he had a flashlight, which was a good thing because the theater was dark inside and we would have ended up on someone's lap if he had not shown us the way up the thickly carpeted staircase to seats in the balcony. In the first row! In the middle!

"We should have gotten popcorn," Mom said regretfully, "but not enough time today. Next time."

I didn't mind. "I'm full of chocolate cake." But I was thrilled that there might be a "next time."

"It's usually a double feature, but not today," Mom

whispered as we settled in. "This is a special show." As my eyes adjusted, I could see the inside of the Palace Theater. And "Palace" was the right name. It was spectacular, with intricate, gold-studded paintings and designs from the floor to the domed ceiling. A giant crystal chandelier hung from the dome's center. Down front on the main floor, a man was playing an organ that sent a deep, resonant sound into the filled theater. The music ended, and another man stepped to a microphone on the side of the stage. His coattails were even longer than the ushers'.

"Ladies and gentlemen," the fancy-dressed man began, "welcome to the Palace Theater. You have been treated to the Mighty Wurlitzer organ. Please give Mr. Bob Kessler a hand for his fine music." People clapped like thunder while Mr. Kessler took a modest bow. "And now for our feature presentation!" the announcer boomed with a flourish. The velvet stage curtain rose ceremoniously to reveal the picture-show screen that took up the entire stage. The theater went black, sound came out of nowhere, and the title flickered onto the screen up front.

For the next hour and a half, I was on a plantation in Georgia with a boy named Johnny. He found out that his mom and dad were getting separated, which was really sad and reminded me of what happened to Billy Tallman from school. Johnny got so upset about the whole separation thing that he decided to run away. But before he really got started on the runaway road, he met Uncle Remus. Uncle Remus was a Negro man who worked at the plantation but was not a slave, and I was glad about that. I remembered the awful coon dogs and what happened to the slaves on Great Grandpa's mountain. I guess the movie story took place after Abe Lincoln's proclamation that freed slaves, but no one ever said.

Uncle Remus was full of stories about Brer Rabbit and the other Brers, and the stories helped Johnny solve his problems. By the end, everything turned out good. Uncle Remus said it was a zip-a-dee-doo-dah day and started walking through the woods, singing:

Zip-a-dee-doo-dah,

zip-a-dee-ay

My oh my, what a wonderful day.

Plenty of sunshine headin' my way,

Zip-a-dee-doo-dah, zip-a-dee-ay!

Butterflies and birds fluttered and flitted everywhere. All kinds of animals started singing and joined the walk-a-long. Johnny and his kid friends skipped out of nowhere and somersaulted down the path behind Uncle Remus. It was the perfect "shake the stink off" ending.

I was still humming the next morning at the breakfast table. "Everything feels lighter," I said to Mom.

"It does," she agreed through her careful smile. "Like there's not a care in the world."

"Like a zip-a-dee-doo-dah day." I grinned.

♦♦♦

The last February surprise came late in the month. I caught Mom and Daddy having a low, so-the-kids-won't-hear talk, and I suspected they were up to something. But what? I couldn't figure. "What were you and Daddy whispering about?" I finally put the question to Mom over dish washing one night.

"Nothing." She kept the secret tight. So later I tried Daddy as I curled in his lap.

"You'll find out soon enough, Sweet Potato."

And I did the very next day. When I came in the door from school, the first thing I saw was a telephone. It perched like a shiny black crow on the table next to the door.

We had never had a telephone. I had never once dialed a telephone. I had never talked on a telephone. Almost no one I knew had a telephone—or wanted one for that matter. And why would they? If you needed to tell someone something, you just went to their house and knocked on the door. Or if they were too far away, like California or someplace, you sent them a letter in the mail and waited for them to write back. What people already did seemed to work just fine, so why did we need a phone?

There were telephones downtown, I knew. When we had first moved to Ohio, I noticed peculiar little buildings on some of the street corners, and I asked Mom about them.

"They're telephone booths." She knew right away because she had been a telephone operator before she met Daddy. "Anyone who wants to make a call goes into the booth and dials zero to get the operator. When the operator comes on the line, she says, 'This is operator forty-four. What number, please?'" Mom used her operator voice and smiled sheepishly. "I was operator forty-four when I worked for the telephone company." I had already guessed.

Mom went on, "When the operator gets the number, she says, 'That will be fifty cents, please,' or whatever it costs. The caller drops the money in the coin slot, and the operator connects the call so the people can talk."

A telephone booth on a street corner seemed like a fine idea if you had to get ahold of someone really fast and if you had lots of change in your pocket, but to my way of thinking, a telephone wasn't really something you needed in your house.

Connie Conklin's family had a telephone, but her daddy owned the furniture store. And a few other kids at school had lines to their houses, but not many. I had never guessed we would become one of them. Mom must have talked hard to get Daddy to agree. I stared warily, almost afraid to touch the new contraption.

"Where did this come from?" My question came out harsher than I wanted.

"I ordered it from the Ohio Bell Telephone Company," Mom replied, surprised by my accusatory question. "The truck came this morning to run the line in from the pole."

"Can we really talk to people on it?" Curiosity was beginning to take over my skepticism.

"Yes, of course," Mom responded softly, disappointed by my suspicion.

"How does it work?" I finally asked the question Mom was hoping for.

"Our number is Franklin 7871." Mom started with the basics. "And our ring is one long and one short." I cocked my head into a question. "We're on a party line with three other houses," she explained, "and each party has a different ring. We only answer when it rings long, then short, so that way we don't make a mistake and pick up on a call meant for someone else."

"Can we call someone right now?" My interest peaked. I couldn't think of anyone to call, but I wanted to try.

She took the receiver from the cradle and put one end to her ear and held the other close to her mouth. "Dial like this." Mom put a finger in one of the holes on the wheel part of the telephone and twirled the dial until it stopped. "If you want to dial a seven, put your finger here." She showed me the numbers painted by each hole. "For an eight, put it here."

"But what if I don't know the number?" I was getting into it. Maybe I could call Connie.

"Then you can dial zero and get the operator. She can help." Mom was proud. "You know that's what I used to do."

"I know." I smiled. I caught her kidding me a little, but I was proud too.

"Also, dial the operator if you want to make a long-distance call," she added. "Maybe tonight after everybody's home, we can try to call Aunt Alice." She twinkled. I saw that she had been hoping for this ever since Aunt Alice sent her new phone number. "And remember"—Mom was back to basics—"before you start dialing, always pick up the receiver and listen to make sure no one else is on the line. If you hear talking, just hang up quietly and wait until they're off." It all seemed like a lot to keep track of just to make a call, but Mom was really happy. She could finally talk to her sisters, and that made the bother worth it.

"Hello, operator, I'd like to make a person-to-person call to Miss Alice Johnson in Annapolis, Maryland." We had all gathered around Mom after supper to try out the new telephone. "Yes, the number is Washington 2964." Mom spoke with clear authority in her old operator voice.

We waited. I could hear the ring come through the ear part of the receiver. "This is operator thirty-six, and I have a person-to-person call from Mrs. R. E. Richardson in Hilliard, Ohio, for Miss Alice Johnson."

"I'm Alice Johnson," a voice responded.

Operator thirty-six to Mom: "Go ahead, please." Just like that, we got to talk to Aunt Alice 500 miles away, and we each got a turn to say hello. Aunt Alice's voice crackled some, but I knew it was her when I heard her "hoot" laugh coming through the receiver. Mom talked the longest, of course, and Daddy the least because talking cost by the minute and he wanted us to "keep it short."

Spring Up, Down, and in Between

March came like a lion and left like a lamb. In between we flew our kites. The field across the road from our house was the perfect spot. Spring wheat planting didn't begin until April or May, depending on weather, so we Leap Road kids had the open field for the whole month of March.

"Can I go when you get your hair cut tomorrow?" I surprised Daddy with the request. Usually I had little interest in following him around Hilliard on his runs into town. They took forever. First we would go to Huffman's IGA to get hamburger (three pounds for a dollar), Fels-Naptha laundry soap, five-pound bags of pinto beans, and anything else Mom had put on the list. We didn't have to get milk or bread from the IGA because the bread man from Donaldson Bakery delivered our bread every Thursday, and the Borden's milk truck brought two quart bottles of sweet milk and a quart of buttermilk to our front stoop every other day.

After the IGA bags were in the Dodge trunk, Daddy usually went to the Farmer and Merchant Bank across Main Street. He paid our electric bill at the window, along with the new telephone bill. If we needed coal delivered, or bottled gas for the kitchen stove, we'd walk to Russell's Feed and Grain on Center Street across from the railroad tracks. Winterringer's Dry Goods was on the way back to the Dodge, and it was the place to buy socks or new work overalls if we needed anything like that.

Willbarger's Drug Store was always the last stop, and the best, because Daddy would buy me an ice-cream cone at the counter in back—a double dip, chocolate on the bottom and mint chip on the top—and that almost made the town trip worth it.

But I didn't have ice cream on my mind when I asked to go with Daddy into town. "I want to go to the Red and White while you're getting your hair cut." He looked surprised. We almost never shopped at the Red and White Grocery.

"It so smells bad." Mom wrinkled her nose and joined the conversation. "What do you need from there?"

"They've got the best kites," I said. "I want a Hi-Flier, and they're hard to find. A kid at school says the Red and White has them for a dime, and that's a really good deal." I added the last part because Daddy couldn't refuse a "good deal."

The next morning I rode in the front seat with Daddy

for the trip into Hilliard. It was only a couple of miles, so we were parked in front of the IGA almost before I got settled.

"Help me shop for groceries, Sweet Potato." Daddy opened his door. "Then it'll go faster." We headed to the meat counter first. It was all the way to the back of the IGA, past the canned vegetables and the heads of lettuce.

"What can I do ya for, Mr. Richardson?" Mr. Huffman stood ready behind the glass display case in his bloody white apron. The case held long metal pans of chicken drumsticks, pork chops, and beef rump roasts. There were three different pans of ground hamburger meat—the eighty-nine-cent extra-lean kind, the fifty-nine-cent lean, and the three-pounds-for-a-dollar kind, which we got.

"Weigh me three pounds of that hamburger, please." Daddy pointed to "our" pan. "And how about that small rump?" That surprised me. We hardly ever had rump roast and gravy, but Daddy had gotten a hankering, I guess. Mr. Huffman laid a piece of white butcher paper across the scales and scooped a mound of hamburger on top.

"Three pounds with a couple ounces over." He looked toward Daddy. "That be okay?" Daddy gave the nod, and Mr. Huffman wrapped the mound in the paper, sealed it with his special tape, and marked the price on the top with his black crayon marker. "Which roast you want?" Mr. Huffman turned to the business of the rump. Daddy pointed to the small lean cut in the front of the case.

"And how about slicing me up a pound of that bacon there?" Daddy tapped the glass. "Looks good and lean."

We left Mr. Huffman with our three meat bundles in hand and began to shop the aisles for the rest of Mom's list. When Daddy crossed off the last thing, we headed up front to see Mrs. Huffman. She was the checker, and Mom always reminded us that we needed to "watch her like a hawk" because she made lots of mistakes on the prices, "always in the store's favor." Daddy put all our items on the counter as expected, but then he did something surprising. He handed each item to Mrs. Huffman one at a time with an announcement: "One can of tomato soup, 12 cents; four apples, 20 cents; two bars of Ivory soap, 35 cents . . ." And so it went. Mrs. Huffman frowned but tapped in the prices without a word.

"There's more 'an one way to do things," Daddy chuckled on the way to the car. He had found his own method to "watch her like a hawk."

We had no bank business or reasons to stop at either Winterringer's or Russell's. "I'll head to Adkins' for a cut." Daddy nodded toward the barber shop. "Clyde'll be busy today, so I'll be awhile. You wanna go on over to the Red and White?" He released me from the boring wait at the barber shop. I scooted across Main Street to pick out the Hi-Flier that waited for me.

The Red and White smelled bad, as Mom had said, but I hustled past the stinky food on the first floor and climbed quickly upstairs. The second floor was a hodgepodge, from dinner plates to batteries, women's girdles to birthday cards. At Christmas I had found a glow-in-the-dark Dick Tracy detective pocketknife for Daddy on the second floor of the Red and White. I had thought it was the perfect gift, and Daddy had said it was, but I hadn't seen him use it, so maybe not.

Dennis, who had put me on to the Hi-Fliers, had said the kites would be in a pasteboard box at the end of the aisle, standing like sticks wrapped in colored paper. I found them right away, but only a few kites stuck out of the box. "Hope, hope, hope." I scanned the meager selection for the Hi-Flier label.

"Ohhhh, they're all gone." I fingered the last of the miserable supply, and then went back through the kite box for a final check. "No Hi-Fliers," I said, talking myself through the disappointment, "but maybe this one instead." I pulled out a blue paper kite with a label covered in butterflies. "Zip-a-dee-doo-dah!" I sang out loud, remembering the final movie scene with dozens of butterflies flitting all around Uncle Remus.

"Did you get the Hi-Flier?" Daddy asked when I got to the barber shop.

"Nah, they were all gone." I acted disappointed. "But they had this one!" And I held up the butterfly kite for Daddy to see.

"That's a fine-lookin' kite, Sweet Potato." Daddy beamed from the barber chair.

"Sure is." Mr. Adkins clipped and snipped while he talked.

I unwrapped the butterfly kite as soon as we got home and spread the blue beauty on the front-room floor. The two wooden strips that made the kite frame were held together by a loose metal ring.

"Rotate the sticks so they make a cross." Jerry came up behind me. He knew more about kite assembly than I did. I took Jerry's advice to make the cross, then hooked the kite's corner strings to the end of each stick. The last one was hardest because I had to bend the short arm of the cross to make a bow.

"Can you help me hold it while I hook the last corner?" Jerry kept the bowed crosspiece taut while I did the final hookup. The butterflies danced all over the blue paper. They were itching to fly. We just had to get the string attached and make a long rag tail to stabilize the kite in the air.

"Mom, do you have something I can cut up for the kite tail?"

Mom washed the last cereal bowl and then dried her hands. "Let's go look." I followed her to the closet at the top of the stairs. It was more of a crawl space than a real closet, but Mom stored the Christmas decorations there along with boxes of old clothes and such. "This should be it." Mom handed me a bag full of threadbare sheets and old towels saved for cleaning rags. "See what you can find there." I wanted colors that would go with the butterflies and dug to the bag bottom before I found just the thing: a bright-blue flowered sheet.

"Got your string on," Jerry announced when I came down with the blue-sheet tail trailing behind. He was heading out the door with his old red kite and an extra ball of string. I tied the tail to my butterflies and followed.

Max and Allen Gray were in the field with Tommy Mere, who lived up Leap toward Jeanette Road. Allen's kite was already almost out of sight, sitting lazily in the cloudless sky. "Not much wind up high," he reported. "Goes easy once you get it past the trees. Anybody got extra string?" I could see his ball was almost to the end.

The field was surrounded by giant elms and oaks, but the field itself was tree free. That was a good thing because nothing ended the fun faster than a kite in a tree. Kite skeletons hung in the branches around the field as mournful testimony. If you took a dive into the trees, you might as well cut the string and go home. But trees weren't the only problem. Overhead telephone and electric wires lined the Leap Road border of the field. So with trees on three sides and wires on the fourth, I walked to the middle of the field. "That's the best place to start." Tommy spoke up when he saw my strategy. "Want me to run it for you?" I knew he meant he would run with the kite to catch the wind while I worked the string out.

"Okay, sure. Thanks." I hardly knew Tommy and was surprised by the offer. I handed him the butterflies and unwound the string to give him some slack. He waited for a gust of wind, and then he started running with the kite high to take advantage of the breeze. I played out the string to keep up.

I could feel the line go taut when the wind caught hold of the butterflies. They flitted and sputtered until the kite took off. Tommy turned it loose, and I let out the string as fast as I could. "Walk backward!" Tommy yelled when he saw the kite hovering perilously close to the elms on the east side of the field. I started backward and pulled on the string to give my kite some extra lift. The butterflies finally cleared the treetops and soared into the blue! I could hardly let the string out fast enough. "Nice." Tommy walked along beside me.

"Wanna fly it for a while?" I offered him the string ball.

"Sure, thanks." He was pleased. I guess he didn't have a kite or had hung his in the trees. We flew the butterflies the rest of the day, and the next and the next, until the tractor came to plow the field for spring wheat.

Daddy got stirred up when he saw the tractor plowing the ground across from our house. "I start itchin' to plant when I see that old John Deere." He rubbed his hands together. "Best tractors ever made," he said in admiration. "Last forever and don't break down—a real workhorse." With that final endorsement, he headed across the road to chat with the farmer in the field. Daddy was looking to make a deal to get our not-yet garden plowed and ready to plant.

I watched Daddy stand outside the fence until the John

Deere dragging the plow came around to lay down another row. When it got close, Daddy threw up his hand in greeting. The farmer returned the wave and held up two fingers to show he wanted to do a couple more rows before he stopped to talk. Daddy nodded and waited.

"Skaggs says he can plow up the garden on Monday," Daddy reported when he came in. "Wish it was sooner, but it was the best he could do. Of course he's gotta plow his own fields first." Daddy was resigned. "We need to get our peas in, though. It's gettin' late in the season."

"It's just the first week in April, Ross," Mom reminded him. She wanted the garden, too, but not as much as Daddy. "We've got plenty of time."

"The earlier, the better." Daddy gave his standard garden answer.

Mr. Skaggs came to plow on Monday as he had promised. I was hanging upside down in the pear tree "draining my brain" when I heard the John Deere putt-putting along Leap Road toward our house. The Skaggs family lived on Jeanette Road in a little place with a big barn out back where Mr. Skaggs kept his tractor and equipment. The family didn't own a farm themselves, but Mr. Skaggs leased several fields on Leap and Jeanette and sometimes off Scioto-Darby Road on the other side of the railroad tracks. He farmed those fields just like he owned them. The real owners got a share of the money from the hay and wheat when it sold.

I somersaulted down from my limb and went to watch the plowing. Even I could tell it was going to be slow going because the land beside the house hadn't seen a garden in several years. The whole acre was overgrown with grass and weeds. Daddy had gone out on Sunday to dig out the sapling oaks and maples that had sprung up in the unattended plot. "Plow can't handle the trees," he explained. "Wanna give Skaggs as clear a ground as we can. It's going to be hard enough as it is." He grunted, pulled, and dug until the trees were gone. "Next year'll be easier."

When Daddy finished the tree digging, he stepped off our garden. "We got about a hundred yards this way"—he pointed from the road to the back fence—"and about fifty yards across. That's a good piece of land for a garden." Daddy was already thinking about where to plant the sweet corn and how many rows of string beans he wanted.

Mr. Skaggs pulled the John Deere to the outer edge of our "good piece of land" and lined up the plow so the first cut would make a straight furrow to mark a trail for the second row. He dropped the sharp, curved plow blades into the ground and moved the tractor forward several feet, where he stopped, set the brake, and hopped down to inspect his work.

"I aim to go down about eight inches if I can," Mr. Skaggs called to me over the tractor noise when he saw I was watching. "That should be enough to turn this sod over and bury it. Gonna take some work, though." Just what Daddy had said. Mr. Skaggs climbed back on his John Deere and ran the eight-inch-deep furrow all along the garden edge to the back fence. He lifted the blades and circled back to the starting point to begin the second row. He positioned the tractor tire in the furrow of the first row, dropped the blades, moved forward a bit, jumped down, checked the work, and adjusted something on the plow before finishing the second row. He repeated the procedure for row after row until the whole garden was lined with furrows of fresh-turned earth.

Mr. Skaggs left the tractor running and came over to where I was standing. "Tell your daddy I'll be back in a few days to disc it. Probably have to run over it a couple times anyway. Soil's pretty packed 'cause it ain't been planted in a while. Looks pretty rich, though." Mr. Skaggs touched the bill of his cap and nodded before he turned back to the John Deere.

I reported it all to Daddy when he got home, and we settled in to wait. But when it came to gardens, Daddy was impatient, so on Tuesday afternoon he got home a little early and we headed into Hilliard. "Come on, Sweet Potato, let's go get some seeds so we'll be ready when Skaggs is done." I liked to work the garden as much as Daddy did—all except the weeding, of course, but nobody liked that part.

"You still got onion sets?" Daddy greeted Mr. McMillian, who came through the narrow aisle from the back of the hardware store.

McMillian's was a two-story brick building at the corner

of Main and Norwich Streets. The top floor was the meeting room for the Independent Order of Odd Fellows. An IOOF sign dangled mysteriously at the top of the staircase that ran from the sidewalk to the Odd Fellows' door. The bottom floor of McMillian's was the hardware store that offered all the tools and free advice needed to fix anything. Drawers lined every wall. They held nails, screws, nuts, bolts, and washers in every size and all manner of other gadgets to hold things together. One aisle was dedicated to painting—inside, outside, wood, iron, even pasteboard, it didn't matter—McMillian's had what was necessary to do the job. Hammers of all descriptions hung on display boards over the shelves in a different aisle. Saws with toothy blades dangled beside them. Screwdrivers—Phillips and flat head—filled the wooden bins underneath, along with wrenches, regular pliers, and my favorite: funny-looking Channellock pliers, each sporting its crooked, bird-like head.

"Sure, plenty of onions left in the barrels." Mr. McMillian directed us toward the back of the store, which was garden central in the springtime. "Got white and yellow." Mr. McMillian followed along, talking from behind us. "Got seed potatoes, too, if you're looking for them. Little late to plant 'em, but still time to get a crop."

"Don't plant white potatoes, but we'll need some sweet potato slips end of May." Daddy reached for a paper sack above the onion barrels. "But this is my sweetest Sweet Potato." Daddy swung his arm over my shoulder to pull me into a hug. "Don't you think she's the finest girl around, Mr. McMillian?" He beamed. Daddy was always embarrassing me like that. I felt bashful and pleased at the same time. Of course, the people he asked always thought I was "the finest girl."

Daddy filled three quarters of a bag with yellow onion sets the size of marbles, then half a bag of white ones. "Might as well get the bean seed and the corn while we're here." He pulled out a few more bags. "And peas and limas," he added. "Your mother's got to have her lima beans." By the time we stepped out of McMillian's, we had every seed we needed to start our new Ohio garden. We'd come back in May for the tomato and green pepper plants and, of course, the sweet potato slips. We were ready to plant!

But before we got to it, something happened that *really* embarrassed me, and it had nothing to do with being Daddy's "finest girl."

"This afternoon we are starting a unit on health," Mrs. Shaw announced after lunch on Thursday. She handed out Dittoed copies of *Your Body and You*, with an outline drawing of a man on the front. The see-through guy showed all the inside stuff it took to digest his food—his stomach, intestines (big and small), liver, and gallbladder. The whole food processing tube from mouth to butt, and everything in between, was etched in the blue lines of the Ditto ink. I waved the sheet close to my nose. Everyone liked the sharp, sweet smell of a Ditto copy.

No doubt, Mrs. S. had put her art skills into action to draw the digestion man onto the Ditto master sheet she used to make our copies. The Ditto machine was in the back of the school office, where no students went, but the repetitive clacking sound would announce when a teacher was cranking out copies of important lesson materials.

"All right, class, take out a sheet of paper." Mrs. S. went on with the lesson after everyone had a copy of *Your Body and You*. "Make a list of what you had for breakfast," she instructed. "Then we'll talk about what has happened to that food since this morning." I wrote down bacon, toast, jam, and milk, plus butter, of course. Toast and jam had to have butter.

"Nancy, please read your list." With that, we started the journey from chewing to "evacuation," as Mrs. Shaw called it, and studied each step to learn how our bodies digested food.

"Now," Mrs. S. unrolled a chart and taped it to the front blackboard, "I need a couple of volunteers to accompany me to the office." Hands flew in the air. "Donnie and Thelma." Mrs. Shaw pointed, and the three of them headed out into the hallway.

"We're back," Mrs. S. chirped after a few minutes, and Thelma and Donnie followed her through the door. Together they rolled a big doctor's office kind of scale into the room— Thelma wheeled one side and Donnie the other. It was the scale that usually stood in the balcony over the gym. "Thank you, helpers." Mrs. Shaw moved the apparatus to the front.

The roller base was a metal square big enough for an adult to stand on with both feet. A crossbar topped a shiny steel post that rose about five feet from the block base. The bar had a pointy slider that stopped on numbers, and that was the part that told the weight.

"Here's where we are going to record our height and weight." Mrs. Shaw pointed to the chart she had hung up front. Every name was listed in alphabetical order, and mine was near the bottom. "Mary, come on up. You get to be first." Mary Angle walked to the front and stepped on the middle of the scale like Mrs. Shaw showed her. "First we'll see how tall you are." Mrs. S. extended a ruler that slid out of the scale's post. "Looks like you are fifty-four inches, Mary. Okay, class, what is that in feet?" She turned to us.

"Four feet, six inches." Several kids knew the answer.

"Good work," Mrs. Shaw praised and entered the numbers 4'6" beside Mary's name on the chart. "Now your weight. Stand still so we can get an accurate read." Mrs. S. gingerly slid the pointer until the moving crossbar was balanced in the middle and stayed level. "Sixty-eight pounds." Mrs. Shaw recorded 68 in bold, black numerals in the designated column on the chart. I could read it from the back of the room.

Billy Baker was the next name on the list. One by one, kids were called to the scale. The chart slowly filled with numbers—4'4" and 59 pounds for Terry Compton, the smallest kid in our class, and 4'7" and 71 pounds for Darrel Haskins, who had the top numbers to that point in the alphabet. The room buzzed with interest and anticipation, but I watched with growing dread. "Graham Potts," Mrs. S. called. I knew my turn was next.

I shuffled forward when I heard my name. Mrs. Shaw extended the ruler to the top of my head. "Fifty-seven inches, four feet nine," she announced, then concentrated on moving the pointer to balance the crossbar on the scales. She touched it to the right, past Graham's sixty-five pounds, and stopped at seventy-five, but the bar was not even close to level. She moved it to eighty, then eighty-five, then ninety, but the bar did not balance. Behind me, the class grew quiet—waiting for the final tally. I could feel the hot red fire of embarrassment climbing up my neck to my face. Mrs. S. touched the pointer to ninety-five, then to the unthinkable 100 pounds, but even the triple digits did not level the scale's bar. One more tap of the pointer, and Mrs. Shaw finally recorded a scalding 102 on the chart beside my name.

By the time Dennis Woodruff's numbers were written in, my humiliation was complete. I weighed more than anyone in my whole class. That's when I knew I was a fat girl, and it changed how I thought about myself for a long time.

First Taste, First Slam, First Suspicions

Mr. Skaggs worked faster than expected, so we were able to plant sooner than we had thought we might. Daddy and I were the garden workers. Mom was the cook for the fresh garden vegetables and the one who would can the extra so we could eat out of the garden all winter, but Daddy and I were the planters, the weeders, and the harvesters during the spring and summer.

"Come on, Sweet Potato, let's get this garden started." Daddy pushed his chair back from the supper table, and we headed out to put our first seeds into the Ohio ground. Daddy started to mark out the rows with his hand plow. The plow looked simple to operate, but its slender metal wheel in front and wide-spread wooden handles in back made it difficult to maneuver a straight, evenly dug row. The hand plow was definitely a Daddy job, and I followed behind him to drop the seeds into the V crevice left behind by the plow's sharp-pointed blade. When I finished my row, Daddy came behind with the plow again to lay another row just inches away from the first so that the soil spilled over and covered the seeds. Onion sets took extra time because I had to push each bulb—root down—into the V, then Daddy did his plow magic again to cover the little marble sets.

"We did a good day's work." Daddy smiled over the results of our labor. "We got in the peas, the lettuce, the kale, and the onions," he told Mom later when we got back inside. He was proud, and so was I.

I knew the harder planting work was still to come. Tomatoes, peppers, and sweet potatoes would go in the ground in late May after frost danger, and that work wouldn't go as fast. For tomatoes and peppers, Daddy would mark a straight row, then hand dig little holes every foot or so along the row. I would come behind and carefully place one seedling and a can of water in each hole. Daddy would bury the roots with soil and gently pack it around each plant. Sweet potato slips would go in the same way, but in a foot-high ridge that Daddy had built up with the hoe.

When we planted the first seeds, the nights were still cold, and frost lay like white fuzz over the grassy fields on many mornings. "We could still get some snow," Daddy reminded me, but hoped we wouldn't. The early vegetables liked the cool, and within days they sprang up in neat rows.

As spring moved forward, the light came earlier and lasted longer into the evening as the sun warmed the ground and coaxed green leaf buds from the elms and slender shoots of wheat from the newly planted field across the road. Our seedlings grew steadily into ever-maturing plants. The peas sent out thread tentacles searching for a place to wind, and we checked daily for white blossoms to appear because the fresh peas in the pod would not be far behind.

"I think we could get some lettuce," Mom announced one afternoon when I got home from school, "and some green onions." My mouth watered because I knew Mom was planning to make wilted lettuce, my favorite spring dish from the garden. Dark blue-green kale was good, too, cooked with a wedge of salt pork and touched with vinegar from the glass cruet on the table, but Mom's wilted lettuce was the best. "Go out and cut us a mess." Mom handed me a paring knife and bowl for the lettuce. "Bring in six to eight green onions too," she directed. "And skin 'em in the garden," she reminded me, but I already knew to cut off the end roots, the tough outer peel, and the tips of the green tops.

"Got the bacon ready." Mom greeted me when I came through the back door, the lettuce bowl in hand piled with curly yellow-green leaves. "Looks like enough." She eyed my work. "Get it washed up good." The whole kitchen smelled of bacon, and a big mound of brown, crispy slices lay draining next to the stove. Mom had navy bean soup and corn bread ready to put on the table when Daddy got home, but the wilted lettuce would be made right before we sat down so it could be eaten straight away.

"Holler Jerry in for supper," Mom called to me from the kitchen when she heard the Dodge crunch into the drive. I was deep into a book about Florence Nightingale, who was a famous nurse. She did a lot to change the way hospitals were run, which was a good thing because back in the 1850s, when Florence Nightingale was a nurse, hospitals were dirty and overrun with rats and fleas. I put Florence down and went to fetch Jerry. My mouth was ready for wilted lettuce.

"Crumble the bacon and onions over the lettuce," Mom directed from the stove when I came in with Jerry close behind. Bacon grease sizzled in the iron skillet. "Stand back," Mom warned. "This'll splatter." She added cider vinegar to the bacon fat, then quickly poured the spitting-hot dressing over the waiting lettuce. The greens wilted down into bacon-drenched deliciousness.

"Best ever, Eva." Daddy complimented the salad. We all agreed the Ohio garden was already a success.

♦♦♦

Spring brought more than kites and gardens—it also brought softball to the school playground. As the weather turned bright and fresh, we squirmed at our desks and could barely wait for recess, when we ran free on the dusty diamond. We had thirty minutes in the morning and thirty more in the afternoon, with an hour over lunch, and we ball players ate fast, hoping to get several innings in before the bell lined us back to the hot classroom. The best diamond was in the field next to the jungle gym and slide. A worn, dusty path marked the baselines through the grass, the pitcher stood in a bare circle of dirt in the middle, and we designated home plate and each base with a sheet of pasteboard held down by a rock. Before each game, one of us had to get the softball and bat from the office where Mr. Moore had his desk. No one had a glove.

"Ready to choose up sides?" Gary asked the group when Thelma and I arrived with the school's bat and ball. No one questioned that Dennis and Gary were the captains. "Let's see who goes first." Gary lobbed the bat up in the air and Dennis caught it with one hand on the way down. He held the bat up with the fat barrel toward the ground. Gary grabbed it just above Dennis' hand, then Dennis let go and placed his hand just above Gary's. They alternated hands up the bat until only the very top of the slender neck showed. Whoever owned the last hand got first pick for his team. Gary got the honors.

"I'll take Donnie." A good choice.

"Roger." Dennis pointed. Also a good pick. And so it went until everyone who wanted to play was selected for a team. I was never picked first, but never last either, because I could bat okay and run like the wind. If I hit the ball, I hardly ever got thrown out on base.

About a week into the season, I surprised even myself and moved up on the captains' "pick list." I was on Gary's team, and we were losing four to three at the bottom of the third inning. Margie was on first base, Bob on second, and Dale waited at third—all good—but we already had two outs. "Batter up!" Dennis called from the dusty pitcher's circle. "Come on, we've only got about ten minutes before the bell." He was eager to get the last out and seal his team's win. I stepped to the plate.

"Strike one!" Mr. Evans, the student teacher, called out from behind me after Dennis' first pitch. Mr. Evans was practicing on us in Mrs. Shaw's class for a month so he could be a real teacher when he finished college at Ohio State. He liked softball, too, and agreed to be our ump during recesses. "Strike two!" Dennis had underhanded the ball to home plate, and Mike caught it and threw it back so Dennis could pitch the third strike. Or so they thought.

Instead, whack! I slammed the ball solid and dead center! I could feel it take off from the bat's barrel, and Dennis barely had time to watch it sail over his head between second and third base. The outfielders never even raised their hands to touch it. The ball kept going and going until it completely disappeared. Dale tore from third to home, Bob crossed the plate next, followed by Margie. Then I skidded over home as a grand-slam hitter!

The moment was thrilling but marred some by the missing ball. "Did you see that?!" Admiration turned to a perplexed "Where'd it go?"

"Into the sheep pen" was the final consensus. The sheep pen was on Mr. Sweptson's farm across the road.

"Game suspended till we find the ball." Umpire Evans grinned and shook his disbelieving head. "Let's go look." He organized five players into a search party, and we fast-walked through the outfield and across Scioto-Darby Road. We found Mr. Sweptson pitching straw in the barn.

"I've never heard of such a thing," he chuckled as Mr. Evans explained the missing-ball situation. "Let's go see." He stood his pitchfork against the wall and led us out to the sheep pen.

"Margie, Bob, Dennis, come in with me," Mr. Sweptson directed. They were farm kids and could be trusted in the pen with the twenty nervous sheep baaing and skittering from one side of the pen to the other.

"Carol, you and Mike help me look in the yard." Mr. Evans was a non-farmer too. We searched inside and outside the pen for close to thirty minutes with no sighting. "We'd better get back." Mr. Evans finally called off the search. "We don't want Mr. Moore to send out a search party for us." He grinned mischievously, but we knew he had checked with Mrs. Shaw before we left.

No one ever found my grand slam ball—the only softball we had for the whole school. We feared our games were over, but Mr. Evans presented us with a brand-new replacement before he went back to Ohio State. Then I knew he was going to be a really good teacher when he became "real," like Mrs. Shaw. Because of him, we still played ball at school every chance we got. Sometimes I even got picked first, but I never hit another grand slam.

◆◆◆

As spring wound toward mid-May, I didn't play softball as much, and Thelma and I often spent our recess time racing around the playground, chasing each other for the fun of it. Thelma was fast, but I was even faster. It was my speed that unexpectedly brought me together again with Mr. Evans' gift ball.

"You'll never catch me," I teased Thelma one Friday morning. We had been cooped up with year-end tests all Thursday and then Friday. Our energy was exploding like Jerry with his firecrackers. I took off down the gravel incline from the school building to the swing set across the playground.

"Bet I can." Thelma turned up the speed and almost caught me by dodging through the swings in a try to cut me off. I managed to keep ahead and raced back toward the outside stairs that led to the gym. The round steel bars around the concrete steps were home base, and I stopped there to catch my breath. Thelma joined me in a pant.

"I'm off." I launched into a dead run again after my

breathing slowed to normal. I sprinted down the gravel incline but took a different route, toward the jungle gym and slide close to the ball diamond. I could hear Thelma slipping in the loose rock and turned my head back to make sure she was okay. She lost some steps but still galloped toward me at full speed. I needed to give my complete attention to beat her.

As I turned my head to the front again, I was met by two barely separated sounds: whack! the unmistakable bat to ball, then thud! as my face exploded in blood and pain.

"Carol! Carol! Carol!" Thelma yelled my name in alarm. Mrs. Shaw rushed to where I stood stunned. Blood ran in a bold, steady stream from my nose down the front of my yellow-and-white plaid. My favorite dress was ruined! I started to cry. For the dress? My throbbing face? The shock of the hit? All of it.

"Let's get you to the office so we can get this bleeding stopped." Mrs. Shaw took charge. She put her arm around me. Mr. Moore was on his way out as we neared the playground door.

"Oh my!" I saw the horror on his face when he caught sight of me. "Oh my!" he repeated. "What happened?"

"Softball" was all Mrs. Shaw needed to say. Thelma was left standing at the door while Mr. Moore and Mrs. S. hustled me into the building. Blood trailed across the playground gravel, through the door, and down the steps to the office.

Mrs. Shaw put me on a cot set up in the corner of the

Ditto room. Even full of blood, my nose caught the unmistakable sweet-sharp odor of Ditto copies. Mr. Moore found a large green towel. "Hold this on your nose," he instructed. The bloody gush slowed to a thin stream, then a trickle. Mr. Moore's face began to relax. "Do the Richardsons have a telephone line?" he asked Mrs. Shaw, then me. "Do you have a telephone at home, Carol?"

I nodded. "Franklin 7871." I was proud that I had remembered our number.

Mr. Moore went to his principal's desk, and I heard him talking to Mom: "Softball in the face. . . bleeding stopped . . . shook us up . . . will bring her home . . . " The last part was what I really wanted to hear.

Mr. Moore pulled his sky-blue Chevy into the front circular drive usually reserved for busses. Mrs. Shaw walked me to the car, where Mr. Moore stood waiting with the front passenger door open. I didn't want to get blood on the cream-colored seat, but he said not to worry—it would wipe right off the Naugahyde upholstery. Mr. Moore chirped about this and that during the two-mile drive to Leap Road, but I didn't feel like chirping back.

Mom met us at the door and stood talking to Mr. Moore while I went inside. I was lying on the davenport by the time I heard the Chevy back down our drive. "We'd better get the doctor out here to make sure you're okay." Mom had decided.

I didn't answer right away because I didn't know how

to say what I wanted. Finally, "I don't want to see Doc Carr." Mom looked at me with a question. "I don't want any of his medicine to make me sleep."

Mom stood silent, then slowly nodded. She understood. "You don't have to take any pills you don't want to," she said softly, "but I do want him to make sure your nose isn't broken." And with that, she went to dial the doctor's office.

"Doc Carr's not doctoring anymore," Mom reported when she got off the call. "There's a new man named Hoeflinger who took over the practice. He's got office hours tonight." I knew I would be going.

By the time Daddy got home, my right cheek was fiery red and swollen, and I knew there was no use making another plea to skip the doctor. Daddy and I went early, but the waiting room was almost full with patients when we arrived. There were no appointments, just first come, first served, so Daddy and I sat down to wait our turn. The room smelled sharply of rubbing alcohol, with no fresh air. No one talked— maybe they were too sick to chat, or maybe the oppressive dark paneling took the cheer away. "Next." Dr. Hoeflinger opened the door that separated his office from the waiting room. An old man got up and shuffled through the door.

"Doesn't seem to be broken," the doctor told Daddy when we finally got our turn. "You're going to have a black eye for a while." He turned to me. And that was it. Dr. Hoeflinger was a man of few words. Daddy reached into his back pocket for his billfold and handed the doctor a five-dollar bill for the visit. For once he didn't try for a "good deal."

◆◆◆

My eye went from red to purple-black to yellow that finally faded to my regular skin color. By the last day of school, I looked normal again, which was good because I wanted to look my best for the Maypole Dance.

"No classes today or tomorrow," Mrs. S. reminded us. She was as excited as we were. "Today we'll turn in all our textbooks and clean up our classroom. Tomorrow is Field Day and the Maypole Celebration *and* . . . " she added for emphasis, "the day we find out the May Queen and King." Only the teachers and Mr. Moore knew who had been selected to be the Queen and King of the May, but we knew it would be kids from our grade.

"Who do you think will be May Queen?" I asked Thelma when we were walking and talking at recess.

"Prob'ly Nancy or one ta' other purdy girly ones," she offered. "One thang's fur sure, 'twon't be me." She smiled wisely and brushed her dungarees. I knew Thelma was right about the last part, but it was a shame because she was one of the prettiest girls in the class. Her long, dark hair glistened in the sun, and her brown eyes were twinkly and serious at the same time. But more importantly, Thelma was kind to everyone and a loyal, thoughtful friend—qualities that should put her way ahead in the Queen race. But we both knew that pretty would trump everything else, especially if the pretty was blonde . . . *And not fat*, I added in my head, knowing without doubt that my humiliating 102 on the scales would preclude me from May Queen consideration.

By nine the next morning, every class had gathered in the open grassy area alongside the school building. We were excited to be freed from desks and "kicking up our heels like fresh colts," as Grandma would say. The teachers rounded us up and divided us into teams for relay races, three-legged races, potato races, wheelbarrow races, and every other race they could think of. Thelma and I were on the same team with six other kids from our grade, including Roger from our class. We voted to call our team the Bandits in honor of Roger's dog, the fastest dog in the world—or so he claimed, though I didn't know how he could determine that. But we agreed it couldn't hurt to be named for a dog mascot that was fast, even if not definitively proven the fastest.

By lunchtime, we were all still kicking, but noticeably less frisky. The Bandits took first place overall in the morning races, and Mr. Moore called us up onto the platform to pin a blue ribbon on each of us. Roger said that when he got home, he was going to pin his on Bandit's collar because, Roger reminded us, Bandit was "the fastest dog in the world" and deserved the ribbon to show it.

"There's no lunch in the cafeteria today," Mr. Moore announced soberly to the hungry bunch of us after the awards ceremony. "But there is a picnic on the grass!" We exploded with cheers and then gobbled hot dogs, baked beans, and potato salad until our bellies hung. And we could go back through the line for chocolate cake if we wanted it, and for as much cherry Kool-Aid as we could drink. Even the Triple M wore a red Kool-Aid mustache when the picnic was over.

Field Day games were fun and the surprise picnic tickled us, but everyone was excited to get to the main event of the afternoon: the Maypole Dance and the crowning of the May Queen and King. Two decorated thrones stood waiting on the platform behind Mr. Moore, and the festive maypole towered over the grassy field. We were ready to begin. "Gather at the maypole," Mr. Moore directed.

Miss Roberts took charge, and we surrounded the pole in a huge circle. And just as we had practiced during music class, each of us took one of the long, colored streamers that hung from the top of the pole. When the lively flute music floated from the speaker, we began to sing and weave in and out around the circle.

All the teachers—even Miss Martin—joined the maypole circle, and we celebrated our last day of school and the beginning of summer in fine style. After several rounds, Mr. Moore entered the dance by catching the hand of Margie Anderson and then Dale King. The rest of us continued to circle and sing, but Margie and Dale followed Mr. Moore to the platform and took their thrones as the Queen and King of the May.

"I tol' ya 'twould be one o' da purdy girly ones," Thelma confided knowingly as we rode home on the school bus for the last time until September.

"Pretty, girly, and one of the 'popular' group," I added. I didn't have anything against Margie, but I was beginning to suspect that the odds were stacked against girls who didn't dress right and girls who topped 102 pounds.

Graves and Cherries

The giant pink peonies and the purple flags came out just in time for Decoration Day at the very end of May. Mom and Aunt Annie—Johnson Clan number one—were pleased to have so many cut flowers for the family graves at the cemetery. Annie lived on Manchester Avenue in Columbus close to the UAW union hall where Daddy went to Sunday afternoon meetings once a month. Sometimes Mom and I would ride in with him to Annie's house, where she would make us lunch in her tiny kitchen and talk with Mom about family news. Annie's husband, Omer, baked bread for Donaldson Bakery and had to work on Sunday, so it was a nice time for the sisters to visit.

On Decoration Day Sunday, Mom and I clipped and snipped long, blossom-heavy stems and loaded them into the boot of the car. Daddy didn't have a union meeting, so we went to Annie's house to collect her and the flowers from her backyard. When the boot couldn't hold another petal, the old Dodge took the four of us to Union Cemetery on Olentangy River Road. The graveyard was filled with hundreds of stone markers—some flat to the ground, others tall and imposing. A confusing maze of roads wound through the acres of carved granite stones, but Daddy never missed a turn. He knew the way to Norma's grave.

"Carol, go help your daddy with the water." Mom handed me four empty coffee cans that she had been saving to use as containers. She and Annie stood at Norma's gravestone sorting the flowers.

"Come on, Sweet Potato, let's get the job done." Daddy headed toward the pump, swinging two empty water pails. By the time we sloshed our way back to the grave site, Mom and Annie had cleaned all the weeds and overgrown grass from around Norma's stone marker. We were ready to decorate. We arranged the flowers in the water-filled cans and secured them to the ground with bent wire clothes hangers. Mom fussed and fretted to get them "right" but gave up in the end. Nothing could really make things right again except for Norma to come up out of the ground whole and well, which of course could not be.

"Let's go to Little Bobby's." Mom gathered the bouquets for the second grave. Little Bobby was Annie's grandson, and he was three when he drowned in the Chesapeake Bay.

"Got pulled in by the undertow," Annie said. "No way to save him." Once when we visited Solomons Island, Uncle Vinson took us in his boat past the spot where Bobby drowned. It was a little rocky beach along the Chesapeake shore where a Saturday afternoon picnic had ended in tragedy. We cleaned and decorated Little Bobby's grave and then went home, leaving two of our family's children behind.

◆◆◆

We ate from the garden all spring and summer and even into the fall. Spring was lettuce, onions, and peas with cream and butter. Summer was string beans cooked with salt pork, limas slippery with butter, spiny cucumbers in vinegar, and green peppers stuffed with hamburger. Fall was sweet mashed turnips, bitter-hot mustard greens with hard-boiled eggs, and of course, baked sweet potatoes.

We had our first corn on the cob in late July. "About two weeks early," Daddy pronounced happily as he slathered his third ear with butter. July also brought tomatoes. Rows of juicy ripe-red globes hung heavy on the vines, guarded by black-and-yellow garden spiders that wove their webs in and out of the tomato leaves.

"Aw, they won't hurt ya," Jerry chided, but no amount of teasing could convince me to stick my hand close to the intricate web. Daddy had warned Jerry not to kill the spiders because they "keep the bugs down." Mom had to pick the spider tomatoes instead of me, but I returned the favor by keeping a sharp eye out for tomato worms. They gorged on tomato leaves until they were fat, green, and hard to spot. Some were covered with white egg-like cocoons that Daddy said had tiny wasps inside.

"We want the wasps," Daddy explained. "They're good for the garden. Leave those worms be." So I avoided the cocoon-covered worms, but I squashed all the others I could find.

Summer was fruit season too. In June we found a patch of wild strawberries in the field, close to the blackberry canes. The wild berries were so small we had to pick for an hour just to fill two quart baskets—enough for dessert, but not jam. "They're just little bitty things," Mom told Daddy at supper. "I wasn't gonna fool with 'em until I tasted one."

Daddy agreed. "Better 'an anything from Huffman's. Sweet and juicy. Reminds me of the ones on the farm." That was Daddy's highest praise.

Our eight acres had two fruit trees, a peach and a pear, but neither one had fruit. "No pollinator trees," Daddy reminded us, "or maybe they're just old and tired." He smiled. We didn't have any fruiting trees, but Mrs. Murdock did. Her cherry was so loaded the branches almost touched the ground.

"You come on over and pick for a pie," Mrs. Murdock hollered across the fence to Mom. She was proud of her cherries. "Or better yet, send Carol. She can climb to the top ones that are out of reach." So I became the designated picker of the "top ones," and truth be told, they were the reddest and sweetest cherries on the tree. "Closer to the sun" was Mrs. Murdock's theory. Mom and I took pails and crawled through the hole in the fence.

Within minutes I was in the treetop, picking handfuls of cherries to fill my pail. I climbed up empty and down full all morning. Mom and Mrs. Murdock worked on the low-hanging fruit—mostly Mom, because Mrs. Murdock was "slowing down," as Daddy said, so she sat in her chair and spotted clusters we had missed. Mom made three pies that afternoon and canned four pints of cherry preserves. She sent me through the fence hole again before supper to deliver a pie and two jars of the preserves.

"What on earth am I going to do with this big pie?" Mrs. Murdock wanted to know, but I could see she was pleased with the gift. "I'm going to my sister's tomorrow for a few days. Maybe I'll take it with me," she quickly decided. I wondered if that had been part of her cherry-picking plan from the beginning.

The sister and brother-in-law came the next morning to fetch Mrs. Murdock, and we watched as they loaded the boot with the pie and a small suitcase. "You all take care of Buster for me." She waved her final words across the fence.

The afternoon lazed along while I stretched out in the glider swing to watch the sky for cloud pictures and consider what to do with the rest of the day. I was tired of reading, didn't want to draw or write, and definitely didn't plan to pull weeds in the garden, though I knew the beans could use the hoe.

"Whatcha thinking about?" Claris Anne's upside-down face appeared above me. I hadn't heard her come up the drive, and I was surprised to see her. She hardly ever came over. Bored, too, I guessed.

"Just watching clouds." I sat up and made space for her to sit down on the swing. We glided and chatted about this and that until I told her about my climb up the cherry tree. Claris Anne's eyes caught a spark.

"Think we could go climb it together?" She leaned forward.

"Right now?" I sparked on the idea too. "Mrs. Murdock's at her sister's, but I don't think she'd care." And with that, we walked to the hole in the fence and crossed the line from our yard into Mrs. Murdock's.

Claris Anne was a good tree climber too. We each gripped a low limb and walked our feet up the trunk until we could swing a leg over the branch. From there we went limb to limb until we reached the thinner top branches that couldn't hold our weigh. That's where we stopped to catch a breath. "We're like spies." Claris Anne peered down through the leaves to the ground. "We can watch other people, but they can't see us. I bet no one would even know we're up here." She lowered her voice.

Silently we watched Jerry come from the back door of

our house, then ride off on his bike. He never once looked our way. Billy Massey stopped in front of Mrs. Murdock's, glanced quickly to see if anyone was watching, decided not, and pocketed a green apple off her tree by the road. For an hour we secretly watched the Leap Road comings and goings from our cherry-tree perch.

When my foot began to prickle, I shifted position and, in the process, broke one of the thinner branches. It dangled in space by a peeled-bark rope still attached to the tree.

"Look at that." I directed Claris Anne's eye to the curly bark peel. That's when we noticed curled starts of bark peel on all the branches around us. I pulled the start closest to me and stripped a long, curly piece of bark around and around until the limb underneath showed shiny green and naked. Then Claris Anne pulled a bark start next to her. And that's how the game began. We competed to see who could strip the longest bark peel. We worked our way down the tree from branch to branch, stripping limbs naked as we went. By the time we got to the bottom, a big mound of curly skinned bark lay at the base of the tree, along with broken branches scattered and wilting everywhere. We stood shocked and speechless. "I better go home," Claris Anne whispered.

"Me too," I answered as we took in the enormity of the damage we had done.

Mrs. Murdock stayed at her sister's house for several days, but I dreaded her return. It was all I could think about.

One minute I hoped that she wouldn't notice the cherry tree carnage, but the next second I knew she would. Her cherished tree was a skinned, diminished replica of its former, lush glory.

Claris Anne and I avoided each other. I didn't tell Mom or Daddy what we had done, and I wasn't sure if Claris Anne had told her parents. No one had seen us, so I decided I didn't have to confess, but I was miserable and ashamed. We had not set out to kill Mrs. Murdock's prized cherry, but we did, and nothing could wind the bark back into place or reattach the downed branches.

"Mrs. Murdock's home!" Jerry slammed the screen door to punctuate his announcement. "Maybe we can go over to watch wrestling on television tonight." When Gorgeous George was in the ring, Mrs. Murdock invited us to watch. She liked the company, and for us it was a special treat. I stood at the open window as Mrs. Murdock got out of the car and waited for her sister's husband to retrieve the suitcase from the boot. She paid no attention to the cherry tree—and then she did.

"Oh my land, what's happened to my tree?!" She threw her hand to her mouth. As fast as I had ever seen her move, Mrs. Murdock was circling the cherry in dismay. "Oh my! Oh my!" Her sister and brother-in-law joined the circle to inspect the dead limbs and dried bark curls.

"What kind of animal would do such damage? Coons

after the cherries, ya think? Possum maybe?" the sister asked.

Mrs. Murdock didn't answer right away, then: "No four-legged animal did this." I could see the truth cross Mrs. Murdock's face. "This was done by kids. Kids for sure," she finished. My heart sank.

We did not watch Gorgeous George on television that night or the next. Mrs. Murdock was not in the mood for wrestling or for company. I stayed in the house to avoid her in the yard. But on Wednesday afternoon, Mom called me over to the conversation she was having by the dancing hollyhocks along the fence.

"Hello, Miss Carol." Mrs. Murdock eyed me. "I haven't seen you around since I got back."

"Hi," I mumbled and picked a hollyhock to act normal.

"Cat got your tongue?"

"No." I studied the white flower but didn't look at her.

"You know anything about my cherry tree?" I shrugged half-heartedly. She knew. "What on earth made you do that?" Her voice cracked in sad disappointment.

"I didn't mean to." I wanted to cry. "I'm sorry," I mumbled. And I truly was.

It was fall before I talked to Mrs. Murdock again. She called me to the fence one afternoon after school to invite us over to watch Gorgeous George on television. Things turned normal again between us after that, and no one mentioned the cherry tree again. I knew then that somehow she had worked it all through and decided to forgive me.

The tree teetered on the edge of death but somehow limped along through the summer. We all watched in silence as the leaves on the stripped limbs turned brown and dropped to the ground. Without the living bark, they had no way to get water from the roots.

So, expecting the worst, I was startled the next spring when I spotted pink-white cherry blossoms bursting out all over the tree. "Daddy! Daddy! Mrs. Murdock's cherry tree is blooming!" I rushed in to share the good news.

"I figured it was a fighter." Daddy smiled. "It wanted to live real bad."

"I wish Mrs. Murdock could see it," I whispered.

"Me too, Sweet Potato," Daddy replied softly, "but I bet she's smiling down from Heaven right now." Mrs. Murdock had moved in with her sister after Christmas because "she wasn't doing very well," and in late January we got word that she had "passed."

"She died in her sleep," her sister told Mom, "and she didn't have no pain." I had never thanked Mrs. Murdock for forgiving me and getting things between us back to normal. I had missed her a lot when we didn't talk. I'd wanted to tell her all that, but I didn't know how. I hoped she'd known it without my saying, and I hoped she knew the cherry tree bloomed in the spring. She would smile about that for sure.

The Ole Mother Cat

In July and August, the garden produced more corn and tomatoes than we could possibly eat. Daddy and I would pick bushel baskets of whichever one was ready and haul them into the kitchen for Mom to put up in jars the next morning. She would start early, sometimes before the sun came up, in order to "beat the heat" of the blistering afternoon. Canning in the middle of summer was hot, sweaty work.

"Water's almost boiling," Mom noted as soon as I finished breakfast. She stood over the sink, washing garden dirt off a tub of ripe tomatoes. "You finish washing the last ones in the basket, and I'll start the scald," she finished.

Before they could be canned, fresh tomatoes went into boiling water for a minute or so until the skins began to crack. Then the whole peel would slip right off. "Nothing nastier than to find a tough old tomato skin in your chili" was Mom's opinion. There were probably nastier things than a tomato peel in chili, but when it came to canning, Mom was the Tomato Queen, so no one bothered to question.

Mom scalded the tomatoes and I skinned them. "Oops! Oops, again!" I muttered as the hot tomato balls slipped out of my hands onto the kitchen floor. When my bowl was finally full, Mom dumped the skinned tomatoes into the pot to heat. The giant canner stood on the next burner and bubbled with quart jars, lids, and metal rings that would hold the lids on the jars while they sealed. Vegetables vacuum sealed in the glass jars would last all winter without spoiling.

"Let's get this batch in the jars." Mom gingerly lifted one of the sterilized quarts from the boiling pot. She used metal tongs to manipulate the glass jar from the hot water and set it upright to receive the steaming tomatoes—all without burning herself or touching the jar. "Quart number one." Mom positioned the flat lid on top of the filled jar and then screwed on the ring to hold it in place. But we were not done. The filled jars had to boil in a water bath for another forty-five minutes.

"Set this one on the towel," Mom directed when the water bath was done. By the time the bushel basket was empty, eighteen quarts of deep-red tomatoes were lined up on the kitchen table. "Listen for the seals to pop," Mom reminded me. As the jars cooled, the lid seals popped into place. Any jars that didn't seal had to be dumped out and reprocessed in the next batch. But that didn't happen often. Mom, as I said, was the Tomato Queen of canning.

Mom canned corn too. Daddy pulled the ears, I shucked, and Mom cut the corn off the cob. She would stand an ear upright and slice the kernels off from top to bottom. Each ear took five or six slices to get all the corn off the cob. "Don't want to waste any." She tossed another bare cob into the basket.

The day was steaming, but the corn couldn't wait. "Open that, will you, Carol?" Mom nodded toward the door between the garage and the kitchen. "Let's let in every breath of air we can." Sweat dripped off our foreheads. "No water bath for the corn," Mom explained. "We have to process it in the pressure canner or it'll go bad. It's okay for tomatoes because they have acid in 'em. Sweet corn doesn't. That's the difference." Mom had grown up canning and she knew her stuff.

We'd been working all morning, and the last pints were in the pressure canner. Only a few nubby ears rolled around in the bottom of the basket. "Not big enough to fool with," Mom determined. "Take those out with the shucks and throw 'em in the garden." I turned to start the cleanup.

"Oh, Mom! Look!" A scrawny calico cat crouched in the corn basket, hungrily gnawing on the nubby ears.

"My land!" Mom shared my surprise. "How on earth did that cat get in here?"

"Must've come in through the garage," I guessed. Mom

and I stood watching in amazement. The cat didn't look up.

"I never saw a cat eat corn on the cob," Mom observed. "She's so poorly, probably starved to death." I heard the soft sympathy in her voice. "Put down a bowl of cream, Carol. She can't survive on corn nubs." And that's how we got The Ole Mother Cat, though we didn't give her the name right away.

At first I feared someone might claim the cat and want her back. "I don't think she belongs to anyone," Daddy said, "and any person who'd let an animal starve like that doesn't deserve to get her back." Then I knew she was ours to keep. The Ole Mother Cat looked like a stained glass window of orange, black, and white. Each color was distinct and vivid. We fed her cream and meat scraps, and tuna juice when we opened a can for tuna noodle casserole, and within a week she began to look like a new cat—clean, shiny, and satisfied. "She knows how to purr." Daddy smiled as The Ole Mother Cat wound her way through his legs. "She had a home before and someone who loved her." Daddy had changed his mind. "You can tell she likes people. Not a real stray. Maybe she just got lost somehow."

Not long after the corn-nub cat had come to us, Mom stood looking at her as she purred away on my lap one afternoon. We'd had the calico only a couple of weeks, but she had already settled into our family. "I wonder." Mom came to my side to inspect closer. "Mmmmm," she said, "I think we got a bunch of kitties in this bargain, not just one."

"What'd ya mean?" I looked up.

"I mean the cat's going to have babies," Mom said simply. Then I noticed the puffed-out belly. "Maybe she's just fattening up," I said, but I secretly hoped Mom's suspicion was right.

"Nah, kittens," Mom replied with certainty and walked away. "I figure another month or so." Mom threw the estimate over her shoulder. I looked at our cat with new respect. She was going to be a mother.

The kittens were born a few weeks later, as Mom had predicted. "There are five in the litter," Daddy reported when he finally got a good look under the front-room bed, which mama cat had decided was a safe spot to have her babies.

"We need to move them to a new place." Mom didn't want the kitten nest under her bed because "they'll start to stink pretty soon." Immediately I went to the garage to find a box . . . and a blanket . . . and a pair of scissors to cut away one side of the pasteboard to make a door.

By the time I finished the box alterations and installed a fluffy blanket, Daddy was back on his knees by the bed. He reached under and brought out a kitten. It was so tiny, like a puffy breath in Daddy's hand. "Looks just like the mama." He handed the fuzzy ball to me. "Did you find a nice, quiet place for the box?"

"In the kitchen closet," I replied softly. Daddy nodded approval. The kitten's eyes were scrunched shut, and Daddy said it would be at least a week before they opened. The kitten blindly nosed my palm, didn't find what she wanted, and issued a faint meow of protest.

"Wants her mama." Daddy watched. "Better get her settled so she can get something to eat." The second kitten was black with white patches, like an Ohio Holstein cow. Kittens three and four were orange-striped tabbies. "Two tomcats," Daddy pronounced. "Orange tabbies are always toms, and calicos are always girls."

Daddy had a hard time finding the last kitten, and when he brought it out, I knew why. It was the smallest of them all. "Runt." Daddy passed the tiny puff of black to me. "Probably won't make it. Bigger ones will root it out of its share of the titty milk."

The black kitten was half the size of the others, but right off I could tell the runt was a fighter. He nosed my palm determinedly and sent up a not-to-be-denied meow. "Hello, little Blackie," I whispered, "let's go find your dinner."

I was right about Blackie being a fighter. From the beginning he latched onto his mama's teat and settled in for a long nurse. I watched over him in the early days to make sure he got his share of milk, and he grew into a shiny black purr machine. If I sat on the davenport to read, Blackie plopped on my belly. If I went upstairs, he meowed at the closed door until I scooped him up on the way down. Blackie was my cat.

"We need to get rid of these kittens," Mom announced

one morning a few weeks later as she dodged around the two tabbies careening through the kitchen. "They're all weaned now and ready to go." Mom was right. The kittens were eating on their own, but I dreaded giving them away, especially Blackie.

"I'll put a Free Kittens sign up at the shop," Daddy said, "and in the store windows in Hilliard." So that was that. The first interested family came two days later—a mom, dad, and two little girls. They oohed and aahed, tickled and cuddled, and finally took the calico that was a replica of her mom and one orange tabby tom.

"Two down, and three to go," Mom noted when the family backed down the cinder driveway. "Where's Blackie?" she asked absently. A daddy showed up next. He wanted a surprise birthday present for his son.

"Boy just loves cats," the dad explained. "Needs one of his own. Good way to learn responsibility too." He decided on the spunky orange tabby. A farmer showed up next looking for a "good mouser" for his barn. The only remaining mouser we could locate was black-and-white "Patches." The farmer was happy to get a cat that matched his cows.

"Blackie disappeared again?" Mom eyed me suspiciously. "He seems to know when to hide." Somehow Mom was on to me. Every time someone came wanting a kitten, I stashed Blackie in the outhouse where no one could hear him yowl. Maybe he didn't like the stink or the spiders or both. But after

Mom's comment about Blackie knowing when to disappear, there was no more talk about free kittens. I guess Mom and Daddy decided, without saying, that Blackie was mine for keeps, and we settled into being a two-cat family.

Until: "My land, that cat's going to have another litter of kittens!" Mom's sharp eye caught the belly bulge before anyone else. After that, we started calling the calico The Ole Mother Cat because we'd hardly give away one litter before she'd start working on another. Maybe she felt lonely without babies.

Trouble and Worry

Other things were going on in our family besides cats. Late summer brought two different and confusing events: one had to do with something Daddy told me, and the other a strange thing Mom did. And I sensed the two things were connected in a way I could not understand.

Daddy's pronouncement came first and was as alarming as it was unexpected. It was a Saturday and unusual because Daddy didn't have overtime work at the shop. The day broke, cool and rainy for August, and the garden had the look of fall. Summer tomato plants lay exhausted on the ground as they rushed to ripen their last fruit before frost. Cornstalks drooped in the wet, stripped of their glorious ears and waiting to dry to crackling Halloween shocks. Cucumbers and green beans had finished their summer work, and only sweet potatoes remained. Daddy and I would have dug them if not for the rain. "Not good to dig them up now," he explained over breakfast. "We want to store them dry so they won't rot." Sounded right to me, and I was glad to put off the task. "Wanna run the dogs instead, Sweet Potato?"

"Sure." I brightened. Running the dogs meant turning Bess and Blue loose in the field behind the house. Daddy and I would follow and roam the eight acres together while the beagles brayed their resonant we-smell-a-rabbit bark. We hadn't run the dogs since the fall before.

"First I have to make a trip into Hilliard." Daddy scooted his chair back to get up. Mom turned from the sink to give him "the look" but didn't say anything. Daddy pretended not to notice. I could feel the tension rising between them. "You be ready when I get back, Sweet Potato. I won't be long."

Daddy's prediction proved wrong as one hour turned into two, but a book on Amelia Earhart held my attention for most of it. She was the first woman to fly solo across the Atlantic Ocean, and then she tried to fly around the globe at the equator. But her plane went down in the Pacific Ocean, and she was not seen again. Mrs. Shaw had said Amelia Earhart was a woman "before her time" because she did a lot of things that women weren't supposed to be able to do, and she made other women believe they could do things too.

I put down the book and wandered into the kitchen to see if Mom had anything she needed me for, but she was distracted about something and sent me away. Finally I heard the Dodge crunch into the driveway. "You took a long time, Daddy," I complained mildly. "I'll go get the leashes for Bess and Blue."

Daddy met me at the doghouse, and I could see right away that he had his swimmy-eyed, rosy-cheeked look that meant he had been to Sparkey's bar while he was in town. We leashed the beagles and headed to the field. Bess and Blue strained against the rawhide until Daddy finally unhooked them past the second fence. The freed hunters stuck their noses to the ground and started off on the trail of some unseen animal scent. Soon we could hear their full-throated brays. "They're tracking something." Daddy cocked his head to the sound.

We walked slowly along the fence in the general direction of the barking until we came to the back boundary of our eight acres. "Let's stop here for a while." Daddy lit a cigarette and leaned with his arms draped over the fence wire. He blew out a big puff of gray smoke that drifted off into the wind. "Things aren't good between your mother and me, Sweet Potato." He took a long draw on his cigarette and never looked at me. I followed the smoky wisps that floated upward from his mouth as if from a dream. I didn't know what to say. Was I supposed to ask what was wrong? Or take his side against Mom? I had no idea what they were so mad about. All of it seemed too big for me to take in, and I knew there was more, so I waited.

Finally, Daddy broke the silence. "If things don't change, I'm going to leave." He turned to face me, and I could see the watery glaze of his blue-gray eyes. Had I done something to make Daddy want to leave? Was it my fault somehow? He said no more and I had no response. I just wanted his words to disappear into the air like his cigarette smoke.

◆◆◆

I did all I could to forget what Daddy had said in the field, but I could never make the fear that clutched my heart go completely away. As time passed, Mom and Daddy hardly spoke to each other, but Daddy got up to go to work every morning and came back home every night. Mom made breakfast and hung clothes as always, and we stumbled along as a family one day at a time doing "normal" things.

And one "normal" was shopping for school clothes— an ordeal I despised. Mom, who loved to shop, hated it too. "Let's get the early bus, Carol," Mom suggested without enthusiasm. "We'll need time to find anything." She was tired from it already.

The next morning we boarded Mr. Jollif's bus to go downtown and rode in silence to Town and High Streets. F. & R. Lazarus loomed before us like a fortress we had to conquer, so Mom straightened her hat and we headed to the sixth floor: Girls' Dresses. I needed size fourteen, but only certain styles would do. We started to search through the hanging dresses on the rack. "How about this?" Mom held up a drab navy blue with a white collar. "Dark is better because it's slimming." Pretty didn't matter; Mom's objective was to find something that disguised my 102-pound body. I was already miserable, and we had just started.

I thumbed past the frilly pinks that the other girls at school looked so good wearing, and I rejected the soft, green-and-yellow plaids. Plaids "make you look bigger," Mom said. She pulled out two dark, plain choices, one forest green and the other burgundy, both ugly. We took eight dresses to the fitting room to try on. "Too tight," Mom rejected. "Hikes up on your belly." Another cast aside. "The pleated skirt makes your hips look big." And on it went until all eight were discarded because not one was "right."

A store clerk flitted in and out to see how we were coming. "Do you have any chubby sizes?" Mom finally asked.

"Well," the clerk considered, "we have just a few. There's not much call for them, you know." What she meant was that not many girls my age weighed 102. I turned to hide the red that flamed my cheeks. Mom was ashamed, too, but said simply, "Would you please bring us what you have?"

The day wound on through the same torment. We scoured all the floors in Lazarus that stocked dresses in my size, then headed to Morehouse Fashion across High Street, then to J. C. Penney several blocks away. Not even a chicken dressing lunch in the Colonial Room could dispel the gloom.

I was afraid to eat for fear of adding one more ounce to my already shamed body. Why did I have to be fat in a world where everyone else was normal?

"Looks like you had a good day shopping." Daddy made his upbeat comment when he eyed our plain brown Lazarus bags. We met him at Hudson and High on his way home from the shop. He knew there was something unhappy about school-clothes shopping, but he didn't understand the extent of my distress.

"We found a few things that will do" was Mom's short, exhausted reply. I was mute on the subject. Daddy didn't ask more.

I hung the five dresses in my wardrobe upstairs and shut the metal door. I didn't want to look at them anymore until I had to select one for the first day of school. Little Blackie clawed his way up the bedspread onto the bed and waited to be petted. I stroked his satiny fur and let his purr soothe the ragged edges of the day. At least the shopping was done for the year.

Or so I thought. "You need school shoes," Mom announced later as she surveyed my worn-out oxfords. "And socks and underwear," she finished. "We'd better go back downtown tomorrow." I figured it might not be too terrible to shop for shoes. At least my feet weren't fat.

The search for footwear went smoothly and turned out okay. We went to Buster Brown Shoes, where they had a florescent X-ray machine and salesmen in starched white shirts and suits. "May I help you?" A tall man met us as soon as we came through the door.

"We're looking for school shoes," Mom replied.

"Right this way." The salesman bowed slightly with his formal reply. We followed him to the back of the store to a boxy machine in the corner. "Just slide your feet into those holes at the bottom, young lady." He directed me to the box contraption. "Now look through the viewing window on the top." He pointed. "Mother, you can look here." He showed Mom a glass panel on the side. It was a wonder! I could see right through my shoes and foot skin all the way to the bones in my feet. I wiggled my toes and watched them move inside the outline of my shoe.

"Let's try a size five," the salesman concluded from the X-ray picture. "Please have a seat." Buster Brown shoes were the best, Mom believed, and they did last all school year, but they were brown leather oxfords with ties—"baby shoes" in my opinion. Some of the girls in my class had started to wear flats or penny loafers or black-and-white saddle shoes. I wanted flats, or at least penny loafers, and tried to convince Mom I was old enough to graduate from the brown lace oxfords.

But Mom said, "Not this year," and that was the end of it. The salesman went to the shelf to select my size. He set the shoe box on the floor beside me and ceremonially removed my old shoe, picked the new one from its tissue-paper wrapping, loosened the laces, and slipped it onto my foot.

"How does that feel?" he asked without a smile. Selling shoes was a serious business. And I had to admit that the new shoe was comfortable, even if it wasn't a flat or penny loafer. "Stand up and walk around," the shoe man directed. When I returned from my walk-around, the salesman poked the top of the shoe to locate my toe. "Seems to be plenty of room." He indicated that Mom should join in the toe poking.

After the shoe box was in the bag, Mom and I crossed back to F. & R. Lazarus for lunch and underwear. Daddy had to work overtime, so we caught the three-thirty bus at the stop on the south side of the F. & R. Lazarus building. When we boarded, we were surprised to find a strange driver behind the wheel. "Where's Mr. Jollif?" another passenger asked.

"Sick" was the terse response. Clearly the substitute was not pleased to be called in to drive the afternoon run. Town and High, where we got on, was the last pick-up stop, and the bus was already crowded with passengers. All the regular bus seats were full, so we took one of the side benches in the front that faced the aisle. The last person to board was a tall, dark-haired man with a mustache. He flashed a friendly smile at Mom and sat down directly across from us. Mom flashed her own quick grin. The driver pulled from the curb and we headed toward home.

"You from Hilliard?" the dark-haired man asked Mom from across the aisle as we rumbled over the Scioto River Bridge, headed west.

"We just moved here from North Carolina about a year ago," Mom responded. "You?"

"Came from Texas to look for work," the man replied. "You know about any jobs?" He stretched his long legs across the aisle, and leather cowboy boots peeked from under his dungarees.

"Work's hard to find." Mom was sympathetic. "What kind of work do you do?"

"Lots of things." He smiled. "I'd take what I could get. That's a fine lookin' girl you got there." He changed the subject and nodded at me. "What's your name?"

I told him, then he went back to talking to Mom. And she enjoyed it. I could tell by how much she smiled. The woman beside us got off at the Mount Carmel Hospital stop, and the man shifted over to sit beside Mom. They chatted away, and somewhere before we got to the Hilltop neighborhood off Broad Street, the dark-haired man in the cowboy boots put his arm across the back of Mom's seat. He almost had his arm around Mom, but not quite. They stayed that way for the forty-minute ride to Hilliard, where Mom and I got off by the vulture mailbox on Leap Road.

I soon forgot about the man on the bus in the last-minute scurry to get supper on the table. But I spotted him again a few days later as he got off the three-thirty bus by our vulture and came walking up the cinder drive. "Oh my land." Mom clasped her hand to her mouth when she saw the cowboy boots headed to the house. Daddy was at the shop, and Jerry was down the road with the Gray boys. Just Mom and I were home. "Quick, Carol, run and lock the kitchen door! Shush." She touched her finger to her lips as she whispered directions. I heard the lock on the front door, then Mom joined me by the kitchen sink. "Under the table." She pointed, and we both crawled into the hiding place. Again she placed a finger to her lips so I wouldn't ask the questions that showed in my eyes.

Rap. Rap. Rap. Three quick knocks at the front door. Mom's hand touched my arm so I didn't move. Rap! Rap! Rap! Louder, more persistent. Then silence until: RAP! RAP! RAPPITY RAP! on the back door, just a walk across the floor from where we were hiding. We didn't breathe for fear of giving ourselves away. A shadow crossed the kitchen window, hesitated a moment, stopped. The dark-haired man was looking in! We stayed folded in our hideaway. The shadow finally moved past the kitchen to the front-room windows and around the side of the house. We waited, frozen to our spot under the table. No more knocks. No more shadows. Mom's breathing slowed to normal.

"I think he's gone," she finally whispered, and we crawled from hiding. "Not a word to anyone about this." No explanation, just a warning. "Not. One. Word," she repeated in her "Johnson Eye" voice so I would know how serious she was.

Dance Lessons

School started up again, and that's when I found out that Thelma had moved. The orange worm gobbled up all the Leap Road kids early on Tuesday after Labor Day, and I saved the seat beside me for Thelma. I hadn't seen her all summer, and we had a lot of catching up to do. But when we neared her house, Thelma was not out front waiting, and the bus rumbled on by without slowing down. The grass was knee-high in the yard, and the garage-house was hollow from the front window all the way through to the back.

"What happened to Thelma?" I asked around at school. No one seemed to know, but Mrs. S. thought the Rigsbys might have gone back to Kentucky or maybe moved to southern Ohio, where they had family, or perhaps Akron, where Thelma's daddy had gotten a job, maybe. No one really knew for sure, but she was gone, and school would not be the same without my best friend.

At the First Day Back assembly, Mr. Moore called off the classroom assignments, and I got Mrs. Shultz for homeroom. So did Connie and Carla, and I was glad because next to Thelma they were my best friends. The three of us lined up together with our new class and followed Mrs. Shultz out of the lunchroom and up to her third-floor room in the old part of the school building, where we chose side-by-side desks across the front three rows. When everyone was seated, Mrs. Shultz stood up front to call roll from her student list. "Billy Baker?"

"Here," came Billy's high-pitched crackle.

"Connie Conklin?"

"Present." Connie raised her hand from front row center.

"Carla Feldpausch?" Carla reported her presence, front row by the door.

"Bob Fox? Nancy Good? Mike Gray? Gary Johnson? Don Rager? Wanda Rapp?" Mrs. Shultz intoned, moving alphabetically down the list. "Carol Richardson?" I raised my hand from the front row by the window.

Mrs. Shultz paused and looked up. She was short and crazy haired. Her fuzzy gray mop stuck out at odd angles on her head, like she had come straight to school from her bed. Black-framed glasses dangled down her crinkly neck onto a soft, saggy bosom, and she perched the bifocals on the end of her nose to read. "Mmmmmm." She considered. "Connie, Carla, and Carol. And all in the front." She shifted her gaze to look from one of us to the other. "Looks like the Three Cs have arrived."

We had Mrs. Shultz for homeroom and English, and her Three C pronouncement was a first hint of her quirky ways. She was often humorous and satirical, mostly unfathomable, and always unpredictable. She liked to "change things up," as she described it. In English class, she might speak to us in verse for the entire class period so we could "get the feel for poetry." The next day she'd have us spend the period writing a 200-word essay about what we ate for supper the night before. "I want to see the colors on your plate. I want to smell the aroma of the food. Make me taste the salty and sweet. Did the bite crunch or mush in your mouth? Details, writers! Details! Give me the details!" That was what she always said. Mrs. Shultz made class interesting because we never knew what was coming, but maybe it was a good thing we didn't have her all day. She was exhausting in a funny way.

Mrs. Nash, in contrast, taught us very precise, by-the-book arithmetic in the morning and ran a strict, don't-dare-even-to-whisper study hall after lunch recess. Mrs. Harsh dished out civics and social studies—one in the morning and one in the afternoon—and a new teacher, Mrs. Boker, tried to interest us in science, but mostly failed.

After the first week, I determined that school was different from what it had been just a few short months before. For one thing, we had different teachers for different subjects, and we changed classes every hour to move from one teacher's room to another. School was still about lessons and tests, books and maps, but more and more it was also about who wore dainty little Capezio T-straps or who had black-and-white Spalding saddle shoes. I had neither, of course, because my Buster Brown tie oxford "baby shoes" were what Mom thought I should wear.

Along with talk about who wore the right shoes also came the giggled and snickered conversations about which boy you liked. And the corollary question: which one maybe liked you. I figured my 102 pounds pretty much eliminated me from the last part, because what boy would like a fat girl, especially one with glasses? But that didn't keep me from having a secret answer to the first part. I definitely had a crush on Gary Johnson. In Mrs. Nash's don't-say-a-word study hall after noon recess, I opened my notebook to the last page, where no one looked, and secretly drew hundreds of hearts with initials inside—C. R. + G. J.

"Who do you like?" Connie asked me over our baked spaghetti and green bean lunch the third week of school.

"Nobody." I kept love to myself and rushed to change the subject. "And what about you, Miss Conklin?" I said in my teasing voice. It was obvious to everyone that it was Dennis Woodruff. And Dennis liked her back. Connie blushed her reply.

All during our conversation, I darted my eyes to where

Gary sat with a bunch of boys from our class. They belly laughed, fidgeted, poked fingers at each other, and soft-punched like boys did. Gary got up, grabbed his tray, and started to the garbage cans to throw away his trash. He was done eating and in a hurry to get all the recess time he could. He liked softball as much I did, so I wasn't surprised to see his glove hanging on his back belt loop. When he was free of his food tray, he slipped the mitt on his hand and fast-walked to the outside stairs that led to the playground. "You wanna play, Carol?" He held up the glove nonchalantly as he passed Connie and me still at the table.

"Sure, which diamond? Side or front?" All natural sounding. I was not self-conscious about softball.

"Side," he yelled over his shoulder.

"Oooohhhh," Connie giggled when Gary was out of earshot. "Sure, Gary, I'll play." She used a mocking singsong voice. "Gary and Carol sitting in a tree, k-i-s-s-i-n-g . . ."

"It's just softball." I tried to convince her, but my cheeks burned.

From then on Connie knew my secret, and she wouldn't let it alone. She just had to know if Gary liked me. Secretly I hoped, hoped, hoped he did, but I acted like it didn't matter one whit if he did or didn't. However, unbeknownst to Connie or anyone else, I cleverly implemented my timed lunch-tray strategy. My plan meant that every day I would just "happen" to be at the dish-room window about the moment

Gary was putting his milk bottle in the drainer. Then—sort of together—we could head down the back steps to the play-ground for the ball diamond. We played softball most every lunch recess all fall, and Gary never seemed to notice nor mind my timed appearances every day.

Despite my protests, Connie remained determined to uncover Gary's "real" feelings for me, and school pictures gave her just the opportunity she was looking for. The traveling photographer came in mid-October to take pictures of each student and a class shot that included the homeroom teacher. He would set up his tripod camera behind the curtain on the stage in the lunchroom auditorium, and we would be called down one class at a time to line up for a turn to sit in the picture chair. The photographer would hang a white fabric curtain behind the chair to serve as a backdrop, and one at a time he would coo and joke us into pasting on a fake grin while he clicked.

Mom had been enthused by the school picture possibility because it would be "professional" and not one of her haphazard shots with the Kodak box camera. "Let's pick out a dress that will look good." She opened the metal wardrobe where I hung my school clothes. "What about this?" She pulled out a maroon dress with a collar. "No, too dark." She rejected it before I could answer. She fingered through the hangers, stopping at each one to consider how the dress top would show up in a picture. "This one," she said definitively and pulled out the dress with the navy skirt, white top, and yellow piping around the collar. It was the best choice; I could see that too.

◆◆◆

The next morning was cool, and as I was about to leave, Mom handed me a white long-sleeve cardigan sweater to wear to school. I buttoned it all the way up to keep my neck warm. "Now don't forget to take off that sweater before you get your picture taken," she reminded me as I went out the door for the school bus.

A spiffy group gathered in homeroom for the morning rituals—the girls especially had taken extra care to look good for the camera. Even Mrs. Shultz had put aside her just-out-of-bed hair and come to school almost combed. The morning classes plodded along slowly as we waited for our call to the auditorium. The summons finally came halfway through Mrs. Boker's uninspired explanation of photosynthesis, and we fled the room in a haphazard line. The photographer's assistant herded us into order when we reached the auditorium and called us forward one at a time in well-honed efficiency.

"Your hair looks so cute." Connie brushed a frizzy stray off my forehead. We were two spots away from the picture chair, and Carla was next in line. She had piled her long, dark waves into a movie-star style, with one side drooped over her right eye. It made her look older, and I wasn't sure what I thought about the effect. Maybe I was a tiny bit jealous of her glamor. "We're next." Connie pulled softly on my arm as we inched forward. Connie went first and smiled admirably when the shutter clicked. A winning shot for sure. I sat down nervously while the photographer pulled Connie's plate from his camera and replaced it with a new one.

"All right, young lady, sit up straight. Let's see your smile." The man behind the camera peeked around to flash encouragement in my direction. I felt stiff and fake but dutifully turned up my lips to expose my front teeth. "Hold it right there." Click, click. "Next." It was over so fast.

Connie and Carla waited on the other side of the curtain, as planned, and it was then that I realized my mistake. "Oh no!" I wailed. "I forgot to take off my sweater!" I peered down miserably at the white cardigan, buttoned up like a straightjacket around my neck.

◆◆◆

It was nearly two weeks before we got the packets of school pictures to take home. I had almost forgotten they were coming, or maybe I just wanted to put the sweater fiasco out of my mind. Mrs. Shultz passed out the sealed envelopes during last period right before the bus came, but I waited to open mine in secret on the ride home after the kid next to me got off. I broke the seal and tore into the envelope. Out spilled twenty duplicate wallet-size pictures of a fuzzy-headed, fat-faced, buttoned-up girl staring forlornly at the world. The fake smile didn't work. Mom hated it. But Connie thought my picture was cute, and she wanted one— she wanted to use it to test Gary.

The weather turned into frosty November, too cold for softball, but Gary and I still quick-talked sometimes in the tray line when I could time it right. He wanted a new ball glove for Christmas, and he showed me his Yogi Berra baseball card. "Best catcher ever!" he exclaimed. "Plays for the New York Yankees," he added. "Me and my dad try and listen to the games every Saturday when they're on."

Early in the month, Mrs. Shultz decided to "change things up" and rearrange the homeroom desks. It took all period to get everyone situated, and when it was done, the new seating dispersed the Three Cs and gave me a view of the classroom that included Gary. Mrs. Shultz stood in front of the room, her revised seating chart in hand, barking out directions like a general on a battlefield. We dutiful soldiers scooted our desks across the wood-plank floor to the spots she designated. Carla moved to the window row in the back next to Bob Fox where, she later reported to us, it was fun because she could talk and pass notes without Mrs. Shultz seeing. We suspected that Carla and Bob liked each other, but Carla didn't let on that Bob was the note recipient.

Connie stayed in the middle row but scooted midway back where—lucky ducky—she was right behind Gary

Johnson. I sat three-quarters of the way back in the first row, which left me well positioned to scan most of the class without being detected. I tried not to pay Gary any special notice, but there he was, right in my eyes, every time I gave my rapt attention to Mrs. Shultz as she paced in front of the room. The new seating suited Connie, too, and while Mrs. Shultz was busy collecting lunch money every morning, Connie took full advantage of the opportunity to strike up regular conversations with Gary. I wasn't sure I liked that, but she assured me that she was just warming things up for the big ask.

After a week, Connie decided that things were warm enough so she steered the morning conversation to the class photo sheet that had miniature school pictures of each of us in alphabetical order. My cardigan button-up shot was wedged between Don Rager and Judy Stevenson. Gary was turned sideways in his seat with one elbow on Connie's desktop. "Your school picture was really good." *Connie had a nice lead-in*, I thought. "Will you sign my class sheet? I'm trying to get everyone," she added, and that was true.

"Sure." He took the pen and photo sheet from her and scrawled "Gary Johnson" across his picture.

"Everybody's picture is pretty good." Connie took back the signed sheet. "Don't you think?"

"Sure." A whatever-you-say reply.

"Whose do you think was the cutest?" Connie persisted.

"Boys aren't cute." Gary's eyes narrowed a tad.

227

"Okay, well, which girl picture is the cutest?" Connie went direct.

Gary nailed her with a "gotcha" smile. "Aw, you're just tryin' to find out who I like."

"Okay, so then who do you like?" There it was. Connie put it to him.

"Hmmmm." Gary put his finger on his chin as he pretended to think. "I'm . . . not . . . tellin'." He spoke slowly and shook a teasing finger at Connie.

"Oh, come on, Gary, who is it?"

Gary glanced unexpectedly in my direction, and I dropped my eyes too late. "Okay, I'll tell you this much." He focused on Connie, but I knew the words were for me. "The initials are not C. R." My heart dropped into my bubbly, fat belly.

◆◆◆

But C. R. were the favorite initials of a different boy in my class. I just didn't know it yet. If boys drew secret hearts in their notebooks like girls did, then Billy Baker had a B. B. + C. R. inside the ones he doodled. The Virginia reel gave Billy the opportunity to reveal his secret love to everyone, including me, and I was mortified.

"Today we are going to dance," Miss Roberts chirped to our afternoon music class. "Boys, you will need to find a girl partner." Alarm rippled through the room. No one moved. Some boys still thought they'd get cooties if they touched a girl, let alone held her hand to dance. Some girls felt the same about boys, but not as many. Then there was the tall/short thing. Most girls were tall. Most boys were short. Mom had said the boys would eventually catch up, but the catch-up thing hadn't happened yet. In the meantime, what girl wanted to dance with a boy's head under her chin? And what boy wanted some girl towering over him? And some, like me, just didn't want to be humiliated if no one chose us.

"Okay, students, on your feet." Miss Roberts chirped on, ignoring our awkward reluctance. "Up! Up! Push all the chairs against the wall so we can have some space to move." Wood scraped on wood as we scooted furniture across the wavy, well-worn floor. Clearly lots of other kids had suffered through their first dance lesson in the music room.

"Okay, boys, line up here." Miss Roberts extended her right arm. "Girls, over here." She threw out her left arm. "Now turn toward the center," she instructed after we had formed the separate boy and girl lines. I pivoted to face the boy line, where I found Billy Baker positioned right across from me, and that meant we were partners. I had yet to understand that it was not an accident. Billy had a plan.

"All right, class, Dennis and Connie are the head couple." Miss Roberts pointed to one end of the line, where my friend and her partner stood happily waiting. "They start the dance because they are closest to the music." Miss Roberts made her way to the Victrola record player on top of the piano. She removed a twelve-inch folk dance record from its pasteboard sleeve and fitted it on the turntable. After the Victrola got the record spinning, she very carefully laid the needle on the first groove to start the music. Lively fiddle notes floated out into the room, and even in our anguish it was hard to hold our feet still. "This is called 'The Rattlin' Bog.'" Miss Roberts was always the music teacher. "It's an Irish folk tune. See if you can get the rhythm." She drummed her pencil to keep time with the music.

That afternoon, Miss Roberts taught us how to do-si-do around our partner and hold hands for the "forward and back." And she made us practice the "swing your partner" part of the reel, which meant a boy actually put his arm around the girl and held her hand while they did some fancy footwork together. It was fun and distressing all at once. Maybe if Gary had been my partner I would have enjoyed it as much as Connie and Dennis or Carla and Bob. Both couples were flushed, hot from the dance or maybe just thrilled at holding hands. I wasn't sure. But I *was* sure I didn't want to do-si-do with Billy Baker. I definitely did not want to hold hands with him for the "forward and back." And I absolutely did not want Billy Baker to put his arm around me to "swing your partner." But everywhere I moved, there he was like a shadow.

"I think he's cute," Connie whispered as we made our way to Mrs. Harsh's social studies class. After music class, everyone knew that Billy Baker liked me.

"Shhh!" I was annoyed. I wanted to dance with Gary Johnson, who played first base better than anyone. I did not want to do-si-do with short, fat, glasses-wearing, silly-grinning Billy Baker, who had followed me down the hall until I escaped into the girls' bathroom.

The "shadow" was with me for the whole next week—on the playground, in the hall, at lunch. I made Carla and Connie promise to go with me everywhere, with one on each side. "He's looking," Connie teased as we forked pork and beans from our plates. Billy was at the table across from us, and I could feel him staring even when he wasn't. For days I refused to glance his way. I returned his hallway "hi" with tight lips and a quick flick of my hand. I knew I was being mean. I surely understood how bad it felt to like someone who didn't like you, but I was mean anyway.

Finally, Billy Baker gave up on me. He scratched out C. R. and instead put P. S. in his secret notebook hearts. P. S. was Patty Snowden, and as it turned out, she liked him too, so it worked out for Billy in the end, and I was glad. It was hard to be mean to him. He didn't deserve it. But things didn't work out as well for me with Gary Johnson, and I stopped writing his initials in my notebook. I decided that Gary just didn't want a 102-pound, glasses-wearing girlfriend, no matter how well she played softball.

The Strike

During the Billy Baker debacle at school, there were unexpected developments at home: the United Auto Workers Local 30 went out on strike. Daddy was grim-faced and determined when he told us about it. "Union took the vote this morning, and it was unanimous." He smiled at that part. He was one of the Local 30 leaders and served on the bargaining committee that tried but failed to reach an agreement with the Columbus Auto Parts Company. An agreement would have prevented the strike, but "the company wouldn't give us what we need, so we walked out."

"Seems like the right thing, Ross." Mom and Daddy were speaking normally to each other again, and I was glad. Whatever had been bothering them in the summer seemed to have settled down some. "How long you think you'll be out?" She was already worried about money.

"Hard to say," Daddy replied. "Could go on past Christmas, I guess. Company might push it that far 'cause they think the men will cave in and go back to work without a new contract so they can get Christmas toys for their kids." I knew it might be a hard Christmas if Daddy was on strike. "But ole man Klages is dead wrong on that one. We won't cave!" Daddy was adamant. We knew Daddy didn't think much of the company owner. "Stuff costs more every day—food, gasoline, rent. We need a raise just to keep up. Klages is making plenty, and we should get our fair share."

He went on: "We're the ones doin' the work and we're only getting a buck twenty-five an hour!" Daddy was riled. I figured his language was about to get "colorful," but it didn't. Mom's Johnson Eye was holding it in check. "Steelworkers union just got a seventeen-cent increase. We're going for twenty-five cents more an hour! Maybe the walk-out will make Klages take us seriously. Maybe get 'im back to the table."

Our family talked union talk all the time, so I knew the "table" Daddy mentioned was the bargaining table where the union leaders like Daddy and the people from the company met to figure out a contract. The contract was a set of rules both sides agreed to.

"The basics are this." Daddy kept it simple when I asked. "The contract says how much the pay is, how many hours we work without a break, and what safety precautions there are so we won't get hurt. There's more, like vacations and raises and overtime, but pay and working conditions are the most important."

Daddy reached for his cigarettes. Mom frowned. Daddy had been smoking more, and the doctor had told him to quit or at least cut down. He blew out a stream of smoke. "After the bargaining committee comes to an agreement, the union members take a vote. If they think the contract's okay, then we sign and go back to work under the new rules."

"Pretty simple," I said lightly.

"Simple, but not easy, Sweet Potato," Daddy replied wearily. "It's a lot of hard work and can take a long time," Daddy measured his words, "and the union guys have to stay together to the end. If they don't, the company will break us and they'll win. It's like matches." I cocked my head in question. "Like matches," he went on. "One match is thin and easy to break. But if you have a hundred matches together, it's a thick bunch and you can't break 'em. Same with the union," Daddy finished. "It's called solidarity." I had seen that word before on the cover of Daddy's UAW magazine. I understood that it meant sticking together no matter what so you'd be stronger.

The shop shut down while the union was on strike because there were no workers to run the machines for the production line. But even though the shop was closed, Daddy went in every day as usual. He spent his time at the union hall or on the picket line guarding the gates to the shop.

Daddy was full of strike talk every night over supper,

and he'd get especially riled when he'd spent the day on the picket line. "We can't let them send in a bunch of Scabs," Daddy steamed. "Taft-Hartley gives ole man Klages the green light to bring in non-union Scabs, but first those lowlifes gotta get by our union guys. And you can bet we won't let 'em past the gate. We'll stop 'em at the picket line! Scabs got no right to our jobs!" Daddy slapped the table in anger. He believed that company owners and their politician cronies in Washington plotted to destroy the union with the Taft-Hartley legislation. And he knew that some non-union workers were low enough or desperate enough to take a union worker's job, and that would take the union's strike power away.

"If the Scabs get in the plant, ole man Klages will get the production line rollin' again. He'll pay the Scabs next to nothin', and we'll be out of our jobs." Keeping the non-union Scabs out was serious business.

Even when Daddy spent the day in the union hall instead of on the picket line, he was full of talk about the strike. "Without a union contract to protect us, the company makes the rules," he'd say over and over. "I know. I've worked in places with no union. The boss pays you as little as he can, then he decides when you're gonna work, where you're gonna work, how long you're gonna work. And a lot of 'em don't care if you get hurt doin' it, as long as they can make more money."

Daddy stopped to catch a story. "One 'a the guys at the shop used to be a coal miner. He said the miners always

235

knew where they stood with the bosses. If there was an explosion and men got trapped underground with the mules that pulled the carts, who do you think the owners saved first? The mules! That's what that guy claimed. Mules were worth more to the bosses than the men." I thought of Thelma's coal-miner daddy. "That's what I'm talking about, Sweet Potato: without the union, the owners'll cut every corner they can just to make another buck for themselves. You got no say over any of it. They even tell you when you can pee."

"Oh, Daddy, they can't tell you when to pee," I giggled.

"Yes, they can, Sweet Potato." Daddy was very serious. "If you don't have a union, you have to do what the bosses say or they'll fire you . . . unless you quit first." His voice was bitter. "That's why we gotta be Union Strong, Sweet Potato, Solidarity Forever!" He smiled to lighten the talk and then scooted his chair from the table to take supper out to Bess and Blue.

Life went on pretty much like always while Daddy was on strike except that we ate more pintos and less hamburger meat and never rump roast. Mom didn't go downtown to shop, and Daddy tried his best to cut down to a pack of cigarettes a day "because they aren't cheap, and we can use the money other places."

"And," Mom put in, "the doctor told you that every cigarette you smoke is like driving a nail in your coffin." Pretty grim stuff, but I believed it was true when I heard Daddy's hack, hack, hacking cough first thing every morning. "You're killing yourself with those cigarettes, Ross." Mom was worried, and Daddy wanted to quit but couldn't seem to. "They got a hold on you." Mom shook her head. Mom smoked too, but just one or two cigarettes over coffee in the morning not like Daddy's two packs a day.

The strike wore on toward Thanksgiving with no end visible. The workers wanted to be back doing their jobs—the owners were losing money every day the plant was closed—but both sides held their positions. "Ole man Klages won't come back to the table," Daddy reported. "And we can't negotiate a settlement if they won't sit down with us."

Each day that went by made it more likely that the impasse would drag on through Christmas. Every Friday, the union paid each worker some money from the Strike Fund, which had been put aside ahead of time, but the Strike Fund pay was just enough to cover rent and food. It helped, but it wasn't the same as bringing home a real paycheck.

◆◆◆

Daddy was getting worn out, but he was steadfast and always thinking of ways to save money. That's why he bought the cow. "I got a really good deal." He tried to sell Mom on the idea. "Farmer was thinning his herd. Says she's a good milker. We can quit the milkman." Mom was not convinced.

But I was excited about having our very own cow graz-

ing peacefully over our eight acres. She came to us on an early Saturday morning in November. "Come on, Sweet Potato,
farmer's here with our cow." Daddy rousted me out of bed
for the delivery. Mr. King maneuvered the trailer to the back
gate, where the collapsed shed had been. Daddy had built
a sturdy lean-to in its place so our cow would have a cozy
shelter. On Friday night, Daddy and I had covered the floor
with several inches of straw and made sure the water and
feed troughs were full. We were ready.

"Gonna be tricky gettin' her out." Mr. King eyed the
trailer. "She's upset by the ride and actin' up some." I could
see a tawny brown cow waiting warily in the bed of the trailer.

"We can do it." Daddy was confident. He knew how to
handle cows.

"Come on, Bossy, let's get to it." Mr. King was all business when he talked to the cow. Daddy opened the gate to the
back field while Mr. King dropped the ramp on the trailer.
Bossy was facing the front of the trailer and glanced around
at the men behind her. It wasn't a friendly look. She was pre-
paring for battle. "Gotta back her out," Mr. King noted. "Not
enough room to turn her around. I'll get hold of her lead." He
climbed up the front of the trailer and reached over for the
rope that tied Bossy to the slat. Bossy butted her head, but
the tether was short, and her horns barely missed Mr. King's
hand. "Dang it, Bossy." Mr. King jerked his hand away.

After several tries and with Daddy's help, they finally maneuvered the reluctant animal out of the trailer to the ground. She really was beautiful, just like a North Carolina cow. Daddy led her to the lean-to and removed the lead from her neck so that Bossy was free to graze.

"She'll settle in after a day or two," farmer King assured. Daddy paid him, and Mr. King hightailed it away. "Don't get behind her." The farmer's last words were a warning.

Bossy took over the pasture. She roamed and grazed all parts, especially the low, grassier areas. Whenever we stood at the fence to watch her, she hustled over. At first I thought she was being friendly, but I quickly discovered that the real purpose was to protect her territory. She would butt at us with her short-cropped horns if we even dared lay a hand or arm on the fence top. I had known Guernseys in North Carolina, but I had never met a mean one. Bossy was a nasty and disappointing specimen.

But Daddy was determined. Every morning before he left for the union hall or picket line, and every evening when he came home, he headed to the lean-to to milk Bossy. Daddy was dogged, but Bossy was just as stubborn.

"Not much to show for it." Mom peered into the mostly empty pail when Daddy returned from milking. Bossy had plenty of milk. Her udder was fat and full morning and evening, and she allowed Daddy to empty her sac because a too-full udder was painful. And Daddy said if he didn't milk her, she'd go dry. "Well, she might as well be dry now," Mom quipped. "We ought to be getting six, eight gallons a day." Mom knew something about cows too.

Daddy stayed grim-faced as he handed her the pail. "She keeps kicking the pail over or stepping in it to ruin the whole bucket. It's like she knows when it's full." He left the kitchen without hearing Mom's final assessment.

"This is hardly worth foolin' with." She swished the meager allotment around in the bottom of the pail.

Truth be told, Mom didn't think any amount of Bossy's milk was worth foolin' with. Having the milk cow created one more job for her. She set a clean, glass milk jar on the counter and fitted her canning funnel in the top. "Where's my cheesecloth?" Mom turned to me but noticed the fine mesh fabric already on the table. She folded the cloth several times, then fitted it into the funnel to make a strainer. "Bring over the milk pail," Mom directed. She began to slowly pour the still-warm-from-the-cow milk into the cheesecloth-lined funnel. The creamy white liquid trickled into the waiting jar. "Okay, we've strained out the hay and cow hair," Mom confirmed. "Let's get this in the icebox to cool." Mom strained milk twice a day if Bossy didn't knock it over or step in the pail first.

I was a big milk drinker, but I didn't drink Bossy's milk. It tasted bad to me, not like the milk the milkman brought. "She must be getting into the hedge apples," Mom guessed.

"I think it's the meanness leaking out," Daddy joked.

Mom tried to convince me to drink the fresh-strained raw milk, but even cocoa powder and sugar couldn't cover the nasty taste. She looked for ways to use Bossy's milk, but with little success. The pudding was bad, and the butter was bitter. Daddy drank the leftover buttermilk without comment but didn't pour a second glass. Mom and Jerry hardly drank any milk, even before Bossy, and I continued my boycott. Jars of milk began to accumulate in the icebox and finally had to be dumped, but Daddy stubbornly took to the milking stool every morning and evening.

"What's this?" Daddy stood in front of the open icebox. We'd had our cow several weeks.

"Borden's milk. Started up delivery again today," Mom said matter-of-factly. Daddy shook his head and closed the icebox door. Mom had given up on Bossy, and Daddy didn't argue. But he still kept milking, determined not to let the cow get the better of him.

◆◆◆

Thanksgiving came and went without either a turkey or another record snowstorm, and kids at school began talking about the Lazarus Christmas window. "It's the best one yet!" Connie reported, and Carla agreed.

Mom fixed wreaths for the door and Norma's grave like always and began a scaled-down version of her usual candy-making frenzy. "Sugar and nuts are expensive," she explained. But even the more modest approach filled the house with the wonderfully sweet smells of cocoa and vanilla. Mom also curtailed her usual Christmas shopping trips downtown. "We need to cut down this year" was her simple explanation. We all knew why. The strike ground on, and we settled in for a low-key holiday. I kept my Christmas wish list to myself.

◆◆◆

"Oh my land! Ross!" Mom's alarm cut through my dream in the middle of the night. It was the second week of December, and Daddy hadn't made it home for supper. He had been on the picket line all day.

"What on earth happened?" Mom again. I made my way downstairs. Jerry was right behind me.

"Scabs." Daddy's one word said it all. The union men had been expecting violence but had hoped it wouldn't come to that. "Ole man Klages is getting desperate," Daddy had told us over breakfast that morning. "We're doubling up on the picket line today."

Daddy sloughed off his heavy jacket and dropped into a kitchen chair. A bloody wound slashed across his cheek, and a round, red goose egg swelled over his right eye. "Things got a little rough today, Sweet Potato." He tried to soften my concern when he saw me looking at his face.

"You need some coffee, Ross?" Mom asked calmly. We were waiting for the details.

"Nah, thanks, Eva." He flashed his gratitude. "Had too much already." He wanted to tell us the story. "Soon as it got dark, ole man Klages sent in a bunch of his agitators and Scabs—musta been a hundred of 'em, maybe more. Brought 'em in the back of dump trucks. They thought they'd just bust right in, start up the machines, and we couldn't stop 'em." Daddy smiled. "They came speeding up, plannin' to smash through the gates, but we were ready for 'em." Daddy flushed with leftover adrenaline. "We had us a line of burning barrels spread across the road . . ." He hesitated, not sure he should tell us the rest. "And . . . and all us union guys stood in front of the barrels in a double picket line to block the trucks." My heart skipped. Mom's hand clasped over her mouth.

"Scabs had to run us over first if they wanted in!" Daddy slapped his fist on the table. "Scab truck drivers thought we'd scatter, but we didn't. Not one guy left the line." I heard the pride in Daddy's voice. "We just stared 'em down and stopped 'em dead." Daddy chuckled. "That made the Scabs plenty mad. The whole bunch of 'em came outta the back of the trucks swinging clubs and chains—knives too." I glanced at the slash on Daddy's cheek.

"Big fight. We won," Daddy said simply to end the tale as he eased back in his chair, pleased with the outcome. "We had clubs too. And we're better scrappers than they are." He grinned. "Beat 'em up. Sent those lowlife Scabs and their hired scum runnin' with their tails between their legs. We won't have any more trouble with them." Then he added, "Ole man Klages didn't know who he was messin' with when he took on our union guys. He's got no right to send in Scabs and thugs to steal our jobs. We're just asking for what's fair."

The story of the fight scared me some, and I knew Daddy hadn't told near all of it. But I was really proud of my daddy for taking up for all of us. The strike wasn't over, but UAW Local 30 was standing strong until it was.

As it turned out, Daddy was right about Mr. Klages getting anxious to start the plant running again. He was losing money every day the machines were down, and when the guys on the picket line fought back to keep the Scabs out, Klages had played his last desperate card. He couldn't break the union with hired thugs, and he couldn't get low-paid Scabs in to start up the production lines again, so Mr. Klages decided to settle. Within a week, the two sides were back at the bargaining table.

"We won!" Daddy announced proudly after two hard days of round-the-clock negotiating. "Ole man Klages agreed to twenty-two cents more an hour and pretty much everything else we asked for. We had him on the ropes." Daddy beamed. "Union guys voted to accept the contract, and we start back to work tomorrow." Relief and exhaustion flooded Daddy's face. "Guess we'll have a Merry Christmas after all." He and Mom exchanged a conspiratorial glance.

The Christmas Magic

With the strike worry over, Christmas plans kicked into high gear. Mom stirred up more candy and made a few trips downtown to shop—but not as many as I would have expected. I went with her for one of the excursions. We spent a long time oohing and aahing over the Lazarus window and had lunch at the Colonial Room. All of Lazarus was decked out for the holidays. Even the sales clerks sported red-and-green elf hats on top of their tight-curled hairdos. "Rudolph" tinkled out of the speakers on every floor, and Burl Ives hoped we would "have a holly, jolly Christmas." "It's hard not to feel Christmassy when you come to Lazarus." Mom happily took in the mood. "Now if we could just convince your daddy to get a decent tree," she joked. We both knew Daddy would still wait to the last minute, hoping to get a good deal.

I had no idea what might be beneath the tree for me on Christmas morning, and I vowed to stay away from playing detective or from peeking through my under-the-bed knot-hole on Christmas Eve. Instead of speculating on what Santa might bring me, I decided to focus on how I could be a Santa myself. I had no cash, but Mom was glad to offer some extra chores, and when I had saved up two dollars, I was ready.

"I need to go to the Red and White by myself," I told Daddy after we parked in front of Huffman's IGA on the regular Saturday trip uptown. I would have rather shopped at Lazarus, but I didn't have enough money for that, so the top floor of the Red and White would have to do.

I hurried through the stinky food aisles and double-timed the stairs to the second floor. Red glass balls dangled from the ceiling on strands of silver garlands, and a Merry Christmas and Happy New Year sign waved like a giant flag from one side of the room to the other. Even the Red and White was in the Christmas spirit. The shelves were packed with an array of gift possibilities, and I had the hard-earned two dollars in my pocket. It would be enough if I was careful.

Red plaid flannel shirts hung from a pole in the men's gift area. Daddy liked long-sleeve flannel, but they were five dollars, so out of the budget. Dick Tracy glow-in-the-dark pocketknives filled the bin next to the shirts. A good choice, maybe, but I had gotten Daddy the same knife already and so passed them by. "Might be okay for Jerry," I mumbled to myself, but I wasn't sure. Then I spied the handkerchiefs. Daddy always carried a white handkerchief in his pocket, and these were monogrammed in the corner. Very special. I searched through the bin for the letter R. The handkerchiefs came packaged three for a dollar, and that was half of what I had.

"What would Mom like?" I wondered. Then I saw the perfect thing—a clear glass deviled egg dish. It would hold twelve egg halves in pockets around the edge, and I knew right away Mom would love it. She liked things to look fancy on the table, especially when company came. Luckily the dish was only forty-nine cents, so I had some money left for Jerry. He was the hardest, I thought, until I remembered the BB gun. He and the Gray brothers had a target nailed to the elm tree out back for target practice, and a roll of 500 copper BBs cost twenty-five cents. Perfect! I had enough and money left over.

"That'll be $1.74 plus tax," the clerk told me when I took my selections to the counter. I pulled two silver dollar coins from my pocket and clunked them down on the counter.

"Don't get these much anymore. Folks usually pay with bills these days." The clerk was surprised.

"My Mom's been saving them for a while" was all I said. I didn't mention the strike or that we were still catching up some and had to dip into Mom's reserve money that she held back for emergencies.

"Find what you needed, Sweet Potato?" Daddy spotted

the white paper bag when we got in the Dodge.

"Yep." I was zip-lipped with my secrets.

◆◆◆

As we neared Christmas vacation, Miss Roberts organized practices for "The Pageant," as she had started to call it. The name had an important ring to it, but as far as I could tell, The Pageant featured the same donkey costume and cotton-ball sheep as the year before. There was a limit to the changes that could be made to the Christmas story. Mary and Joseph still had to get to Bethlehem, and Jesus still had to get into the swaddling clothes.

However, on the last day of school before vacation, Mr. Moore surprised everyone with his unique Christmas present. In addition to The Pageant performance, The Amazing Duncan would do his magic show for us. "Mr. Duncan just recently moved to Hilliard," Mr. Moore told us in the introduction. "He has performed far and wide," our principal expanded, "but today, as a special treat, we have the honor of having The Amazing Duncan right here at Hilliard School!" Mr. Moore concluded with enthusiastic clapping to welcome our guest.

The Amazing Duncan bounded onto center stage wearing a black-tailed tuxedo, a pink silk scarf hanging over his arm. He swished the scarf up by the two top corners, snapped it in the air, and out flapped a white dove. "Oooooh!" He had everyone's attention. For the next half hour, our very own magician found ten quarters, one after the other, behind Mr. Moore's ear, astounded us with fancy card tricks that no one could figure, and made a rabbit disappear from a cage and then reappear from a top hat. He peeled a banana right before our eyes and showed us it was already sliced! He turned water into ice cubes while he poured it into a glass, and he made a metal ring walk up a string from the floor right into his hand. "How did he do that?!" The question rippled through our clapping cheers. Mr. Moore's surprise present was a total success. We started Christmas vacation on a magical high.

Mom was putting up her card-tree decoration over the davenport when I got home, and she taped while I enthused about The Amazing Duncan. "Your Uncle Roy could do fancy things with playing cards," she remembered when I told her about the card tricks. "Not magic so much as tricks to cheat guys he played poker with. He made his living as a gambler, you know." Mom glanced up from her holiday creation. "The gambling and cheating landed him in jail one time." She paused. "Seems I recollect he served six months on the county road gang. We used to see him in his jailbird suit patchin' the road." Mom chuckled her wry laugh. "County made the road gang wear special clothes so they wouldn't try to escape." She laughed again. "Hard to miss a fella wearing a black-and-white striped suit."

Over supper I went on to Daddy about the magician,

and Jerry added the tricks he liked best. Mom retold the story about her "tricky gambler brother" and his jail suit, and we all had a good laugh. Then Daddy said, "Help your mother with the dishes, Sweet Potato. Jerry and I got to go pick out a Christmas tree." We were all surprised—it was still three days until Christmas. An hour later, though, Jerry and Daddy brought home a long-needled Scots pine from Huffman's IGA, and it had only one bare spot, which we turned against the wall.

The next couple of days went quickly. We attended to the usual last-minute details like wrapping presents and baking cookies. "Santa's got to have his Nestlé Toll House favorites," Mom declared, though I recalled who actually ate the Santa sweets. During all the final preparations for Christmas, Mom and Daddy were doing a lot of whispering, and despite my vow to not play detective, I was curious, very curious.

I woke Christmas Eve morning to the delicious aroma of apple turnovers baking in the oven. Mom must have started paring apples right after Daddy left for the shop at six. He would work only half a day and be home after lunch unless, as Mom suspected, he stopped for a "little nip."

"Get your breakfast." Mom greeted me when I arrived, still yawning, in the kitchen. "We have a lot to do." After the toast popped, I lifted a couple pieces of crisp bacon off the plate left over from Daddy's breakfast and slathered strawberry jam on the toast. I laid the bacon between the slices of jam-covered toast to make a sandwich—sweet and salty, the best. "As soon as you're finished, you start chopping celery and onions for the dressing." Mom pointed with her knife. She was washing the inside of a fat roasting chicken. "I want to get everything ready so there won't be so much to do tomorrow." Mom answered a question I hadn't asked, but I wondered about the big hurry.

Daddy got home sooner than Mom had thought he might, but he mysteriously left again right after he and Mom had one of their whisper sessions. What was going on? My detective juices bubbled up.

"I think we've done all we can do today." Mom washed the last bowl and set it for me to dry. "Let's have a little lunch and see if we can find some good music on the radio. They ought to be playing that new Bing Crosby record." She started to hum, "It's beginning to look a lot like Christmas . . ." She paused. "Do you think I can sing as good as Bing?" Mom was in an especially festive mood. I wondered if it had anything to do with the whispering.

Christmas music floated through the house for the rest of the afternoon and into the evening. Daddy returned just as it was getting dark, and the whispering started up again. Mom put on her coat and followed Daddy into the garage. "You kids stay inside," she called over her shoulder on the way out. "And no peeking."

When they came back in, both Mom and Daddy were

all twinkles and grins. Neither Jerry nor I had any idea what they were up to, but we figured we'd find out in the morning.

We huddled around the Philco after supper to listen to the Bing Crosby Christmas Special, sponsored by Chesterfield cigarettes. "Makes me want to light up," Daddy said and patted the shirt pocket where he usually kept his pack of Chesterfields, "but I won't—haven't had one since yesterday." He was trying to quit, but the smokes had a hold on him, we all knew.

"Tonight, special guests Bob Hope and Dorothy Lamour join Bing in a Christmas broadcast to remember!" the upbeat announcer proclaimed. We settled in for an hour of songs and jokes and skits from the three famous entertainers.

"What a show!" Mom and Daddy both agreed when the last song was sung. "That Bob Hope keeps everyone laughing." Daddy was still smiling.

"Off to bed, you two." Mom pointed in Jerry's and my direction. We were surprised by the early bedtime but didn't argue.

"And don't come back downstairs until morning," Daddy put in. Mysterious.

Jerry went to sleep almost right away, but I tossed and stared at the dark. Before long I heard noises below me. The back door opened and closed, then opened again. "Get that, can you Eva?" I could hear Daddy's soft call, then his weighty shuffle across the kitchen.

He's carrying something heavy, my detective-self spoke inside my head. *But what?* While Daddy was outside, Mom was busy in the front room moving furniture. More mystery.

Every nerve in my body was itching to crawl under the bed to the knothole. But I didn't. If Mom and Daddy were going to all the trouble for a Christmas morning surprise, then I wasn't about to ruin it. After a while, the movement in the front room stopped, and everything went quiet. Daddy and Mom had gone to bed, their secret Santa escapades done for the night. I drifted off too.

"I'm dreaming of a white Christmas, just like the ones . . ." Bing Crosby's croon startled me awake, and it took me a minute to question why Mom had the radio on so loud. "Could it be, I wondered?" I sat straight up in bed to see out the window. Bing Crosby—and all of Hilliard for that matter—didn't have to dream anymore. A white Christmas had come gently in the night with several inches of transforming snow! Powdered-sugar flakes decorated the leafless tress, the juniper bushes hung heavy and sparkling to the ground, and a flawless mantle of white overspread the garden and field. Mother Earth had performed her magic.

"You two going to sleep all day?" Daddy was standing at the top of the stairs. That was all the encouragement it took for Jerry and me to hit the floor for a race down the steps. Mom was already waiting in her front-room chair. Everything looked like a normal Christmas morning—lit tree, empty Santa cookie plate, red stockings dangling like fat sausages from their hooks. Everything normal . . . except the blanket-covered boxy thing in the middle of the room. Jerry and I stopped dead to stare.

"Want to see it now? Or wait till after breakfast?" Mom and Daddy teased. They knew the answer.

"Okay, Eva," Daddy said, "you get one side and I'll get the other," and like magicians they lifted the cover off our new Zenith television! Even with my prized detective skills, I never figured it out. Daddy and Mom's Christmas trick was complete.

"Let's turn it on and see what we got." Daddy and Mom were just as excited as we were. "Jerry, help me move this thing to the corner by the electric." Daddy and Jerry maneuvered the bulky, wooden Zenith from the middle of the room to the clear spot Mom had opened next to the wall. That's why she had been scooting furniture in the middle of the night. "We're plugged in and ready to go." Daddy stood up from the extension cord on the floor.

"We can get stations three, six, and ten." Mom knew from watching Mrs. Murdock's set.

"Let's get it on and see what we got," Daddy repeated. He was like a kid, and Mom too. Two knobs stood out under the sixteen-inch circle picture tube—one for off/on/volume and one to dial stations. Daddy turned the knob to "on," and we immediately heard crackling inside the wooden box.

Warming up, Daddy thought, but the picture circle stayed blank and gray.

"What station is it on, Ross?" Mom stooped to look at the numbered dial. "Looks like three," she answered herself, just as a round, spoked wheel appeared on the picture tube. It was black and white with the words "NBC Columbus" at the bottom. Only static rattled from the speaker.

"I'll be . . ." Daddy was disappointed. "Conklin better not've sold me a dud. Try a different station, Eva." Mom dialed the knob to the number ten. Same black-and-white circle, but with "CBS Columbus" listed on the bottom. She dialed to six, but nothing changed except the "CBS" to "ABC."

"I'll be d . . . arned." Daddy stopped his swear, but only because his kids were in the room. He was frustrated.

"I think we're too early." Mom was relieved. She had figured it out. "That's just some kind of test screen. There won't be any real shows broadcast until later," she reasoned. "Let's have the rest of our Christmas and try after breakfast."

And that's what we did. Daddy put one of the monogrammed handkerchiefs in his pocket as soon as he opened the package. "Won't lose track of these, Sweet Potato." He patted the R initial and grinned. And Mom washed the deviled egg dish so we could "try it out for Christmas dinner." Jerry was glad for the BBs, but the White Christmas snow meant he had to hold off on the target practice. Jerry and I got "little things," as Mom called them, because the Christmas money had gone to buy the family television. And the strike had "put a damper on my shopping," she explained, so she and Daddy decided on the Zenith at the last minute, after the strike was settled. That's what all the whispering had been about, and I was glad I hadn't played detective and ruined the tricky surprise.

Fireside Theater was the very first show we watched on our very first television set. It was a special production of *A Christmas Carol* by Charles Dickens. We just called it the "Ole Scrooge Story."

"I feel like I've just been to the picture show," Mom said when *Fireside Theater* was over, "and I never had to leave the front-room davenport."

That Christmas was magical. First The Amazing Duncan, then the overnight snow surprise, and finally Mom and Daddy's television trick. I didn't know it then, but that was to be the last Christmas in the Leap Road house.

Of Cows and Accordions

January folded into February with little of the after-Christmas dumps. The new Zenith television was no small part of that. Every night after supper, we gathered in the front room to watch "our shows," as we began calling them. We each had a favorite.

Jerry liked *Captain Video and His Video Rangers*, and Daddy liked *You Bet Your Life* with Groucho Marx. Contestants tried to answer Groucho's questions so they could win money. It was a lively program. Every week, without fail, a dead duck dropped down on a string into Groucho's face, and the audience never got tired of the gag. Groucho made crazy jokes all through the show, and he always asked, "Who was buried in Grant's Tomb?" Of course no contestant could miss that answer, and Daddy chuckled no matter how many times Groucho asked. It tickled him plenty.

Mom's favorite was *Queen for a Day*. The emcee started every show with the tantalizing question "Would *you* like to be queen for a day?" and all the women in the audience went wild. Of course, who wouldn't want to be queen? Maybe that's why Mom liked the show so much. The emcee interviewed female contestants one at a time, and each one had a really sad story. Maybe one had a sick child, or another's husband had lost his job, so the family had no money. At the end, the audience chose the queen. Whoever got the biggest score on the applause meter was crowned. She got her special wish, like help for her child or extra money until the husband had work. But she also got a lot of other prizes—a washing machine or an electric refrigerator or a closet full of new clothes.

I enjoyed everyone's shows, but the one I looked for was *The Cisco Kid*. The Kid and his sidekick, Pancho, rode their horses all over the West to set wrong things right. In my favorite of the favorite, Cisco got an Indian man out of jail and proved he shouldn't have been there in the first place. The Kid and Pancho had to solve the case fast because it was only a half-hour program.

All winter, the family Christmas present gave us fun evenings in the warm front room while the wind howled and ice glazed the windows outside. Spring edged its way forward almost without our notice, and then it was there.

Light came earlier in the morning and stayed later each day. The icy puddles turned slushy, and then finally: "Mom!

Mom! The crocuses are blooming!" I yelled as soon as I banged through the front door. "They're purple and yellow all along the drive."

"Let me see." Mom slung a light jacket over her house-dress. "It looks like every bulb came up." She was pleased. "I wish Mrs. Murdock could see them." Mrs. Murdock had given us the bulbs in the fall when she thinned out her flower bed. I wasn't sure what to say. I missed Mrs. Murdock too. Losing her after Christmas was our one winter sadness, and I'd feared it would make Mom go to her dark place like the year before, but it didn't.

It was almost nighttime when Daddy got home. I wanted to show him the crocuses, but he put me off. "I got to get to the shed to milk Bossy while there's still a little light. I'll look at the flowers tomorrow, Sweet Potato." He tried to soften my disappointment. Daddy lifted the pail off the counter and took to the cow.

Mom and I had just finished putting supper on the table when Daddy came banging through the back door. He slammed down the empty milk pail and limped into the bedroom to "put on some clean clothes," he snarled from behind the curtain.

"Your daddy's sure hoppin' mad about something." Mom stood poised with a plate of corn bread. We could hear him raging under his breath in the next room.

When Daddy came to the supper table, he was still mad

but calmer. "That's the meanest cow I ever saw," he started. "Ya gotta watch out every minute when you're around her." He forked a crispy ham slice onto his plate. We waited for the rest of the story. "I'm done with her," he finally said between bites. "She kicked me. And it wasn't an accident," he added. "She did exactly what she set out to do." He laid down his fork. "She sent me flying to the other side of the shed. Lucky she missed my head. I won't keep a cow that mean."

Bossy was gone before supper the next day. A man with a trailer came to the door right after Daddy got home from work. He loaded up Bossy and drove away. And we didn't get another cow to replace her. Daddy was done. Bossy had won. But Daddy had the final word, I thought, as I watched the cow trailer go down the drive with Bossy tied inside. Daddy didn't say where she was headed, and I didn't ask.

◆◆◆

We didn't get a cow, but I did get an accordion and music lessons to go with it. About a week after Bossy was gone, Mr. Daley came knocking on our door. He was in our neighborhood "talking to some other families" on our road, he explained, and the other families (never named) had signed up their children to take music lessons.

Mr. Daley was from Daley's Music Studio in Columbus. Their teachers provided "the finest instruction for trumpet and accordion playing," and they guaranteed "to have your child—Carol, right?—playing like an expert within three months." I was hanging on every word. Mom was impressed, and Daddy wasn't home yet. Mr. Daley saw all that and pushed harder. "Surely, Mrs. Richardson, you don't want your child—Carol, right?—to miss out on this opportunity? She has talent. I can see that." How he knew I had music talent was a mystery to me. I didn't even know it myself. The most I had ever done was blow a few screechy notes on a juice harp that I had bought for a dime at the Red and White.

But Mr. Daley was very convincing and even talked Daddy into my talent when he came back for a second visit. He wanted to make sure they had "just the right instrument for the young lady." The right instrument turned out to be the accordion, which was fortunate because accordion lessons were "the Daley Music Studio's specialty," and Mr. Daley just happened to have with him "a fine instrument to leave for the young lady even before she starts weekly lessons." The rental was eight dollars a month plus twelve dollars for the lessons. "All that—the instrument and lessons—for just five dollars a week!" Mr. Daley was excited to offer such a good deal. Mom was hesitant, and Daddy was looking for ways to make the deal even better, but I just wanted to get my hands on the accordion that waited silently for my magic, talented fingers.

"Let's try this." Mr. Daley acted quickly. He sensed the sale was slipping away. "Young lady, you sit right here." He directed me to a wooden chair while he ceremoniously unlocked the accordion case. A shiny black instrument nestled snugly inside the red velvet. Mr. Daley lifted it and set it on my lap. "Now, young lady, put your arms through the straps like this." (He seemed to have forgotten my name was Carol.)

The accordion was a heavy and substantial instrument—sort of like having a little piano on my lap. White and black keys flowed down the right side from my chin to my thigh, and a boxed panel of buttons was fixed to the left. In between was the folded fan of the bellows. Mr. Daley wanted "to give the young lady a quick lesson" to see if I was a "natural." He showed me how to play the piano keys with my right hand at the same time I pressed some of the thirty-one buttons with my left hand. And while I tinkled the keys and tapped the buttons, I pulled and pushed the fan-like bellows that brought air in and out of the instrument to make the music sound. It was hard to do all three things at once, but Mr. Daley oohed and aahed and crowned me a "natural," just like he had thought I would be. Mom and Daddy didn't want to waste my "obvious talent" and signed me up for weekly lessons.

I soon discovered that Edith next door was also "a natural" on the accordion and had signed up for lessons on the same night Mr. Daley signed me. Mom arranged to pay Mrs. Whittle to take me downtown in the Nash to the Daley Music Studio along with Edith every Tuesday night. I guessed that since I had "talent," I could ride with them.

The Daley Studio was in an old brick building on Town

Street several long blocks from F. & R. Lazarus. Edith and I carried our bulky accordion cases up three flights of dusty wood stairs to the top floor where the lessons were given. The "private lessons" turned out not to be so private as four of us "naturals" were crammed into a tiny office with our accordions and our "instructor," who spent most of his time doodling on his pad or staring out the dirty window. "Practice, practice, practice" was the only instruction he had, and he repeated it after each of us fingered and bellows-ed our way through the week's lesson. We puffed out the same off-tune sounds every Tuesday all through March and April.

In May things changed. Mrs. Daley herself took over our progress so we could "prepare for the Daley Music Studio Spring Concert." Instead of four at a time in the tight little office, all the "naturals" came together as one in the main room. "Ready, orchestra." Mrs. Daley lifted her baton. "On the downbeat." That meant we should push, pull, tap, and finger for all we were worth. The result was dreadful. And the sound didn't improve through the whole month of May.

Concert day eventually arrived, and Daddy arranged to be home in time to drive us. The weather was hot and sticky, more like July than late May. All the girl "naturals" had to wear the same outfit—a dark-blue satin skirt with a long-sleeve white satin blouse and black string tie cinched around the neck. The boy "naturals" were required to wear the same but with blue pants. Because I was "so hard to fit," Mom had made my concert clothes by hand. It had taken her hours to stitch the slippery satin into a presentable outfit, but I looked as snazzy as any of the others.

We all arrived at the concert auditorium a half hour early, as Mrs. Daley had warned us to do. Mom and Daddy took seats in the second row from the stage, and I joined the other "naturals" backstage behind the curtain. Mrs. Daley rushed around with her seating chart in hand. "You. Sit here," she barked. "You,"—she pointed—"there." Finally we were all situated with accordions on our laps. Edith and I were front row center.

Seven o'clock came, the curtain gathered up, and Mrs. Daley raised her baton. I could see Mom and Daddy beaming in the audience. The baton fell on the downbeat and the music began. I played with gusto. I punched buttons—any buttons, all the buttons. I fingered keys—white keys, black keys, any keys at random, up and down the board. I pushed and pulled the bellows until I shined with sweat. I had no idea what I was playing or if I was playing any song at all. It didn't matter. I just wanted to look like I knew what I was doing. But of course I did not. Nor did any of us. The "naturals" screeched and scrapped our way through the whole list of titles on the program. Then mercifully the curtain dropped, and we all went home.

Mom and Daddy were quiet on the ride. I didn't want to talk either. We joined together in a conspiracy of silence against the hoax that had been laid upon us. I was not a "natural," the Daley Music Studio was a scam, and we had been sucked in. The satin outfit was nice, though, and I used it for "dress-up" when Claris Anne and I acted out our stories.

The Big Secret

Daddy and Mom were whispering again. I came down early one morning and found them huddled over a bunch of typed papers. Mom quickly folded them back to letter size and tucked the bundle back in the envelope they had come in. I caught a glimpse of the Farmer and Merchant Bank address in the top corner. "Morning, Sweet Potato." Daddy rose from the table and took hold of his lunch pail. "Gotta get going or I'll be late to the shop." He was halfway out the door. Mom slipped into the bedroom with the envelope in hand, and when she came back to the kitchen, she had a hair brush.

"Sit down, and let's get that wool brushed out for school." Mom never brushed my hair anymore. I was too big, but I didn't protest. Mom's newfound interest in hairstyle was my signal to ask no questions about the hidden papers.

School was almost over, and we still had not planted our summer garden. Unheard of! Daddy had kept saying we'd "get to it," but we had never gotten past putting in the early onions and lettuce. Mr. "the-sooner-the-better" hadn't stuck to his own rule to get peas planted by April 15 and tomatoes in the ground by the middle of May. I was truly perplexed, but no matter how many times I asked, nothing more got in the ground.

And The Ole Mother Cat had disappeared. The missing cat and the missing garden had nothing to do with each other, but they came at about the same time. "Kitty, kitty." Mom opened the door and called the calico off and on throughout the day. She had gotten very attached to The Ole Mother Cat and fretted when she didn't come home. It was the mother-to-mother thing, I suppose.

"She's just got her another boyfriend," Daddy assured Mom. "She'll wander in pretty soon, Eva, you'll see."

But she didn't wander in or meow at the door or wrap herself around Mom's legs hoping for a pat and a saucer of cream. "Where could she be?" Mom stared out the kitchen window. Blackie was my special cat, but I missed the calico too. She was the one who had gotten our family into the cat business in the first place. I proposed that we walk the eight acres to search.

"Good idea." Mom was immediately ready, and we set out, calling "kitty, kitty" every few steps. We passed the coal pile, which was almost down to dusty slag. "Well, we planned that pretty well." Mom was pleased that the coal pile had lasted through the winter. We wandered on by the slag, calling "kitty" as we went. We checked the chicory and the Queen Anne's lace around the barrel. The Ole Mother Cat liked to hide in the grass there and wait for mice that nosed their way by. But no luck. I noticed that the trash was burned down to a barrelful of ashes, and I knew Daddy planned to dump them on the garden as fertilizer. But he hadn't "got to it" yet, like the other garden work. The outhouse door hung open and swung back and forth when the breeze puffed by. "Your daddy should fix that lock," Mom said absently as we walked toward Bossy's old lean-to. "Too bad the cow didn't work out," Mom noted between her kitty calls, "but it's all for the best, I think."

We searched every part of the eight acres for any sign of the calico. We passed the wild strawberry bed and checked to see if the plants were blooming. "Looks like a good crop coming." Mom fingered the delicate white blossoms that dotted and dodged in between the green leaves spread like carpet on the ground.

"Blackberry canes are beginning to leaf." I pointed as we passed. "Remember how many berries we picked that first day?"

"And how your daddy just happened to bring home vanilla ice cream for supper?" Mom added. We enjoyed the memory together. So much had happened since our first bowl of Ohio blackberries: Mom's paint job that had made the dreary house bright. The not-yet garden that had transformed into all manner of yumminess. The cow that hadn't worked out. The washed-off witches, and the butterfly kite soaring over the windy wheat field. The long strike and Daddy's union bunch out-scrapping the Scabs. I smiled to think of my still-secret knothole and the unexpected cowgirl outfit. But after that had come the lacy dress and the pills that almost took Mom away.

"Ready to keep looking?" Mom's question cut through my memories. I pushed aside the drizzly fall day when Daddy had told me he might leave us. I turned from the fence to step in beside Mom. She and I shared the secret of the dark-haired man who had sent us under the table to hide. We had never once talked about it after that day. Whatever had been wrong between Daddy and Mom had somehow worked itself out. Our Leap Road family bumped up and down and through stuff—like any family, I guessed. Sometimes we had to get past hard things, but we had lots of happy surprises too along the way. "Just keep puttin' one foot in front of the other, and you'll get where you need to go," Mom often advised, and Mom and Daddy understood that more than most.

◆◆◆

"I think we should have supper in town," Daddy announced when Mom and I got back from our search. I stood speechless with my mouth hanging open. We never had supper anywhere but home.

"What do you think, Eva?" Daddy asked. Mom's lips hinted at a smile, and I knew she and Daddy had planned this little surprise during one of their whispers. "Wha'd ya say we give that M&M Restaurant a try?"

"Just give me a minute to run a comb through my hair and slip on a better dress." Mom headed to the bedroom. "Carol, go change into something clean. You too, Jerry," she directed on her way out of the kitchen.

The M&M was uptown on Main Street between the Farmer and Merchant Bank and Turney's Pool Hall. We took Leap to Cemetery Road and made a right turn onto Norwich Street. Big houses lined both sides of Norwich—close together, but not so close as to crowd each other. And every house had a front porch! Giant trees reached over the street in a canopy that was like driving through a cool, shady cave.

Norwich crossed Main at the IGA, and Daddy parked the Dodge in front of the M&M. I knew kids in my class went there for supper with their families, but I had never been inside. Daddy led us to a roomy booth by the front windows under a sign that promised Home Cooked Food. As soon as we settled, a gray-haired waitress ambled over and plunked a menu down on the table. "Wha'd y'all want ta' drink?" Her cherry cheeks reminded me of Mrs. Murdock, but her name tag said Mary.

"I'll have a Coca-Cola." Mom spoke up like she'd thought about it ahead of time.

"Me too." Jerry and I took Mom's lead.

"I'll have milk." Daddy's favorite. "You don't have buttermilk, do you?"

"Of course." Cherry-cheeked Mary lit up. She was proud to have what her customer wanted. "Y'all new in town?" Mary asked. "Never seen ya in here before."

"Live out on Leap," Daddy replied, "but we're moving."

What?! I jerked my head up in surprise. That was the first I'd heard about it. We were moving . . . again? I glanced at Jerry to see what he knew, but his head was deep into the menu.

I ordered roast chicken with mashed potatoes and dressing and a saucer of cinnamon applesauce on the side. Mary brought the piled plate slathered in gravy. I ate it all, wiped the dish with buttered rolls, and finished the M&M meal with homemade berry pie. Food was my defense against the move that sat like a rock in my belly. Daddy and Mom chatted on about the fine weather and the fine food and the fine service. I just listened.

"Let's walk." Daddy surprised us when we stepped out of the restaurant. "A good meal calls for a little stroll." *Since when?* I wondered. I just wanted to go home and pet Blackie. But Daddy and Mom were already at the corner, and I picked up my pace to catch them. "The O'Briens live here." Daddy

271

pointed to the enormous brick house on Norwich next to the Farmer and Merchant Bank. "Mr. O'Brien is president of the bank," he added. "The Methodist preacher lives there." Daddy nodded his head toward a sprawling white house across the street, next to a little brick church. "Ole man Latham lives here." Daddy continued the Norwich Street tour. "People say he's rich as King Midas." Daddy lowered his voice to a gossip tone. "Works as an auctioneer, so don't know where he got all his money. Maybe had a rich daddy."

We ambled on, and Daddy seemed to know something about almost everyone on Norwich Street. "The Gerhes family lives here. They got a couple of kids, I think." Daddy was talking about the house with a porch as big as a room across the front. "And the Williams family owns this house." We passed a white-pillared place sitting back from the street in the trees. To my eyes, it looked almost like a mansion. I began to enjoy the walk despite my worries. "Old couple and their spinster daughter are the only ones who live there," Daddy added to the Williams family story. "Betty's the daughter's name, and she likes her roses." Beds of stunning bushes lined the walk and the front of the pillared house. "This is the McCoskey place." Daddy indicated the house next door to the "mansion." "Jimmy McCoskey's in your class, Sweet Potato. You know him?" Daddy tried to draw me into the conversation.

"A little," I said, "but he's in Mrs. Nash's homeroom."

"The Springs are here." Daddy pointed to a white house with a black cat lounging on the porch rail. "Don't know much about them."

"They like kitties," I put in as a point in their favor. Mom smiled.

"Cleve Turney, who runs the pool hall, lives there." Daddy flipped a hand toward the house two doors down from the Springs' place. "Nice old guy," Daddy added.

"Who lives there?" I pointed to the house Daddy had skipped. It looked different, with its barn-shaped front, but it had a front porch like all the Norwich Street houses. "Daddy?" Louder in case he didn't hear: "Who lives there?" Mom and Daddy exchanged a smile like a whisper.

"We do." Mom spoke up. "We do."

Before I could speak, Daddy dangled a key in the air. "Let's take a look inside our new house." Jerry's firecrackers took him off to explore the backyard, and I followed Mom and Daddy up the porch steps and through the front door.

"Oh, Mom, it's really fancy!" I breathed, standing in the entry hall with a staircase on the right and wide-paned glass doors on the left. "These are French doors." Mom took hold of the knobs and led us into the front room. A mahogany-and-marble fireplace filled one corner, and three to-the-ceiling windows lit up the other sides of the room. Another set of French doors took us to a huge dining room with a glass chandelier hanging in the center.

The kitchen had an electric refrigerator. "And," Daddy beamed, "the stove's connected to the gas company line. No more propane tanks from Russell's." The new place had a basement for the wringer washer and water-line hookups with spigots that worked. A wicker swing hung at one end of a back porch that spanned the width of the house. The bedrooms were upstairs, along with a real bathroom! With a bathtub! And a flush toilet! But best of all, there were no spiders!

"Let's look out back, Sweet Potato." Daddy and I roamed the backyard that went all the way to the railroad tracks. As we neared the garden spot, Jerry burst from the tool shed. "Wow! This is perfect!" He beamed. He'd already found a spot to hang out with his friends.

The new yard in town wasn't eight acres, or even close, but it was big enough for apple trees that looked good for climbing, a grape arbor, and space for a big dog pen where Blue and Bess could stretch their beagle legs. "Look at this fine dirt." Daddy held up a handful of tilled soil ready for seeds. Then I understood the delay. The garden would be planted at the house on Norwich Street.

We moved the next week, right before school was out. Blackie came with us, but not The Ole Mother Cat. She never came back to the Leap Road house. "Guess she just wants to stay in the country," Mom decided.

I walked home from school the first day we lived on Norwich Street. Betty Williams was on her hands and knees in front of the pillared house when I passed by. Her head was deep in a bed of red rosebuds that would soon fling open their summer glory. No one was home yet at the McCoskey's, but Mrs. Spring stood in her driveway, casting perplexed glances around the neighborhood. "Kitty, kitty," she trilled. "Cat's lost." She smiled my way.

"I can help you look," I offered.

"Oh, thanks, but we don't need to bother." Mrs. Spring waved a dismissive hand. "He'll show up at suppertime." I left Mrs. Spring and settled into our front porch swing to finish my after-school snack from Winterringer's. Carla and I had made a candy run on the way home, and I still had a few pieces left in the bottom of the white bag. Most sweets in the glass case at Winterringer's were two for a penny, so a nickel went a long way. I crunched down on a malted milk ball and watched Mr. Turney's dark-blue coupe putt down the middle of Norwich. He threw up a hand to me as he passed and made a wide turn into his drive. He was home for an early supper break, I guessed, before he took over the evening shift at his pool hall uptown.

Across the way, Mrs. Schatz eased out of her swing and aimed herself for our front porch. She huffed across the street on stout, swollen legs and arrived completely out of breath. "Your mom inside?" She wheezed out the question. Mrs. Schatz was shorter than me by a head and as wide as she was tall. Daddy had said she was from "the old country" and would "take some knowing" but had "a good heart."

"Yes, she is. I'll go get her." I turned to the door.

By the time Mom and I returned to the porch, Mrs. Schatz had settled herself in the swing. "Brought over some preserves." She fished in her apron pocket and handed Mom a pint jar of peach jam. Mom received the gift with a smile and took a seat in the chair. Our new neighbor had come to chat, that was plain.

I sat on the steps for a while, listening to Mom and Mrs. Schatz's getting-to-know-each-other talk, but I finally excused myself and headed around back. The cherry tree was calling to me. It stood tall and strong just below the back-porch steps. I grabbed the lowest branch to hoist myself up inside the leafy branches, where the bees buzzed all around. They were intent on their work because the tree was in full bloom.

Author's Note

Did the *Eight Acres and a Cow* story really happen? The simple answer is yes. The Richardson family—Mom, Daddy, Jerry, and Carol—did move to Ohio in the late 1940s and did live on eight acres in a rental house on Leap Road outside of Hilliard, a village with a population of about 500 at the time. We came to Ohio for work, and Daddy took a job as a millwright at the Columbus Auto Parts where he was a UAW Union leader at the plant. And as I portrayed, Mom did suffer from depression, though I had no name for it then. I believe her darkness was related to Norma's death, which was still very fresh in her mind. Even though Mom found her way through the painful loss in later years, her young daughter's death remained a searing memory throughout her 100 years of life. I remember Jerry as a burst of energy, as I describe, but I have few other distinct memories of him during those Leap Road years. I will leave that story for him to write —apologies, brother. The land, neighbors, and house on Leap were much as I described them, and Mom did paint everything to make it livable.

Did *Eight Acres and a Cow* really happen? As I said, the simple answer is yes in regard to the basic facts. But I add this note especially for my longtime friends and classmates: some events, time lines, and characters in the book went their own way as the story unfolded. Of course, conversations are long forgotten and must be recreated from imagination, but names, dates, and the order of things can be fuzzy as well and need the art of storytelling to fit together. *Eight Acres and a Cow* was never meant to be a strictly historical account— though much of it is—rather, it is intended as the story of one poor family from Appalachia who came to Ohio to make a better life. More specifically the story is a composite and re-creation of one young girl's memories of that family, that life, that time, and those people who populated it.

The 1950 Great Thanksgiving Snowstorm did happen, and still retains the record for the deepest snow in Ohio's history.

Acknowledgments

Many deserve my gratitude for all that came before to make this book possible, but I am especially grateful to my daughter, Heather Dean, and to Marti Alt, my friend and middle school librarian, who took on the task as first readers of the *Eight Acres* manuscript. My son, Eric Dean, played an important role as well. Because of him, I began the journey through the boxes of Mom's photos and keepsakes that inspired me to take on our family's story. I also thank middle schooler Raul Castro Dean, who was the first to hear many sections of the story as it progressed. His enthusiasm kept me at it. And finally, I am profoundly grateful to my partner, Tom Johnson, who is a writer and believes I am one too.

About the Author

Carol Richardson grew up in Ohio and worked nearly twenty-five years in Washington, DC, as a lead grassroots organizer for peace and justice groups. As an ordained pastor in the United Methodist Church, she also served congregations both in Ohio and Maryland. Currently she is retired and living in Columbus, Ohio.

CPSIA information can be obtained
at www.ICGtesting.com
Printed in the USA
BVHW081922060719
552760BV00002B/200/P